THE ONLY INVESTMENT GUIDE YOU'LL EVER NEED

★ A Book-of-the-Month Club Special Alternate
★ A Fortune Book Club Main Selection

"The title is immodest, but the investment advice definitely is not. Tobias's cool, spare, readable style lays bare the rapacious scams of the Wall Street moneymen, and . . . provides a conservative strategy to protect hard-earned savings."

—*New York* Magazine

"Absolutely delightful . . . It's irreverent, rational, sensible . . . Sound advice on how to deal with the whole investment process. Don't let its light touch fool you—it's got more than its share of wisdom."

—*Stock Market Magazine*

"The only investment guide many will indeed ever need."

—*Barron's*

"There comes a point in the reading of any financial guide when the mind collapses. This usually happens around the point when the book starts asking if you've thought of option straddles . . . Andrew Tobias, in his witty and succinct [book], has a pretty sound explanation for these sinking spells . . . It's all a matter of organizing your priorities. And the most basic priority is that before you can start making money through financial investment, you have to figure out how to stop losing money through simple squandering. What Tobias has to say is as rational as a pocket calculator."

—*The New York Times*

"A good primer for anyone who doesn't want to die poor."

—*Washington Star*

"Andrew Tobias is one of the financial community's most pithily perceptive observers."

—*Forbes Magazine*

"Tobias covers the investment market with some down-to-earth approaches that the neophyte should understand easily."

—*San Diego Union*

"What can you say about an investment counselor whose most sophisticated commodities tip is to hoard canned tuna fish under his bed? Has he gone daft? No, he's just practical. And with all the irresponsible investment advice floating around these days, maybe Andrew Tobias is just what we need. His witty little book is for the average Joe. It's funny, readable, and most importantly, it makes good sense."

—*Charleston Evening Post*

"Andrew Tobias, who writes about money for *Esquire,* is a funny fellow but he's also canny and sensible, and his book is well worth its modest price."

—*Boston Sunday Globe*

Andrew Tobias

The Only
Investment Guide
You'll Ever Need

BANTAM BOOKS · TORONTO
NEW YORK · LONDON

*This low-priced Bantam Book
has been completely reset in a type face
designed for easy reading, and was printed
from new plates. It contains the complete
text of the original hard-cover edition.*
NOT ONE WORD HAS BEEN OMITTED.

THE ONLY INVESTMENT GUIDE YOU'LL EVER NEED

*A Bantam Book / published by arrangement with
Harcourt Brace Jovanovich, Inc.*

PRINTING HISTORY

*Harcourt Brace edition published February 1978
6 printings through September 1978
Book-of-the-Month Club edition published February 1978
Bantam edition / February 1979*

*For permission to quote from "Wouldn't It Be Loverly" by
Alan Jay Lerner and Frederick Loewe, copyright © 1956 by
Alan Jay Lerner and Frederick Loewe, the author wishes to
thank Chappell & Co., Inc., owner of publication and allied
rights throughout the world. International Copyright Secured.
All rights reserved.*

*All rights reserved.
Copyright © 1978, 1979 by Andrew Tobias.
Copyright © 1978 by Harcourt Brace Jovanovich, Inc.
This book may not be reproduced in whole or in part, by
mimeograph or any other means, without permission.
For information address: Harcourt Brace Jovanovich, Inc.,
757 Third Avenue, New York, N.Y. 10017.*

ISBN 0-553-12521-4

Published simultaneously in the United States and Canada

*Bantam Books are published by Bantam Books, Inc. Its trade-
mark, consisting of the words "Bantam Books" and the por-
trayal of a bantam, is Registered in U.S. Patent and Trademark
Office and in other countries. Marca Registrada. Bantam
Books, Inc., 666 Fifth Avenue, New York, New York 10019.*

PRINTED IN THE UNITED STATES OF AMERICA

This book is tax-deductible.

To my broker—even if he has, from time to time, made me just that.

Acknowledgments

I would like particularly to thank Sheldon Zalaznick and Clay Felker, the editors with whom I worked most closely for more than four years at *New York* magazine. And also: *New York* magazine for permission to borrow from material I first published there; Carol Hill, whose patience and enthusiasm border on the divine; John and Rochelle Kraus, Laura Sloate, Murph and Nancy Levin, Ken Smilen, Martin Zweig, Burton Malkiel, Alan Abelson, Yale Hirsch, Paul Marshall, Robert Glauber, Stuart Becker, Marie Brenner, Jesse Kornbluth, Don Trivette, Gabriel Perry, and Peter Vanderwicken; *Fortune, Businesss Week, Forbes,* the *Wall Street Journal,* and the *New York Times;* and Texas Instruments, without whose pocket calculator I would be a broken man.

Although much of what I know I have learned from these people and institutions, whatever egregious faults you—or they—may find with this book are strictly my own.

A. T.

Contents

Part One

Minimal Risk

CHAPTER 1

If I'm So Smart, How Come
This Book Won't Make You Rich?

> You have to watch out for the railroad analyst
> who can tell you the number of ties between New
> York and Chicago, but not when to sell Penn
> Central.
>
> —Nicholas Thorndike

Here you are, having just purchased a fat little investment guide we'll call *Dollars and Sense,* as so many investment guides are (although the one I have in mind had a different title), and you are skimming through idea after idea, growing increasingly excited by all the exclamation marks, looking for an investment you would feel comfortable with. You page through antique cars, raw land, mutual funds, flower bonds, Krugerrands—and you come upon the section on savings banks. Mexican savings banks.

The book explains how by converting your dollars to pesos you can earn 12% on your savings in Mexico instead of 5 to 8% here. At 12%, after twenty years, $1,000 will grow not to a paltry $2,917, as it would at 5½%, but to nearly $10,000! What's more, the book explains, U.S. savings banks report interest payments to the Internal Revenue Service. Mexican banks guarantee not to. Wink.

The book does warn that if the peso were devalued relative to the dollar, your nest egg—whatever it had grown to by then—would shrink proportionately. But, the author reassures, the peso is one of the stablest currencies in the world, having been pegged at a fixed rate to the dollar for twenty-one years; and the Mexican government has repeatedly stated its intention not to devalue.

Now, how the hell are you, who needed to buy a book to tell you about this in the first place, supposed to evaluate the stability of the Mexican peso? You can only assume that the author would not have devoted two pages to the opportunity if he thought it were a poor risk to take—and *he's* an expert. (Anyone who writes a book, I'm pleased to report, is, ipso facto, an expert.) And, as a matter of fact, you do remember reading somewhere that Mexico has *oil*—pretty good collateral to back any nation's currency. Anyway, what would be so dreadful if, as your savings were doubling and tripling south of the border, the peso *were* devalued 5 or 10 or even 20%? That would be nothing compared to what happened to you last time round in the stock market.

So, frustrated by inflation and impressed by the author's credentials, you take *el plunge*.

And for eighteen months you are getting all the girls. Because while others are pointing lamely to the free clock-radios they got with their new 5½% savings accounts, you are talking Mexican pesos at 12%.

Comes September 1, 1976, and Mexico announces that its peso is no longer fixed at the rate of 12.5 to the dollar, but will, instead, be allowed to "float." Overnight, it floats 25% lower, and in a matter of days it is down 40%. Whammo. Reports the *New York Times:* "Devaluation is expected to produce serious immediate difficulties, most conspicuously in heavy losses for Americans who have for years been investing dollars in high-interest peso notes." How much is involved? Oh, just $6 or $8 *billion*.

You are devastated. But you were not born yesterday. At least you will not be so foolish as to join the panic to withdraw your funds. You may have "bought at the top"—but you'll be damned if you'll sell at the bottom. The peso could recover somewhat. Even if it doesn't, what's lost is lost. There's no point taking your diminished capital out of an account that pays 12% so you can get 5½% in the United States.

And sure enough, in less than two weeks, on September 12, 1976, the float is ended, and the Mexican government informally repegs the peso to the dollar. (Only now one peso is worth a nickel, where two weeks ago it was worth eight cents.) You may not know much about international finance (who does?), but you know enough to sense that, like a major housecleaning, this 40% devaluation in Mexico's currency ought to hold it for a long, long time. In fact, you tell friends, for your own peace of mind you're just as glad they did it all at once rather than nibbling you to death.

And then on October 26 the peso is floated again, and slips from a nickel to less than four cents. Since Labor Day, you're down 52%.

Aren't you glad you bought that book?

This immodestly titled book (the title was the publisher's idea; in a weak moment I went along) is for people who have gotten burned getting rich quick before. It is the only investment guide you will ever need *not* because it will make you rich beyond any further need for money, which it won't, but because *most* investment guides you *don't* need.

The ones that hold out the promise of riches are frauds. The ones that deal with strategies in commodities or options or gold are too narrow. They tell you *how* you might play a particular game, but not whether to be playing the game at all. The ones that are encyclopedic, with a chapter on everything, leave you pretty much where you were to begin with—trying to choose from a myriad of competing alternatives.

I hasten to add that, while this may be the only investment guide you will ever need, it is by no means the only investment guide that's any good. But, sadly, reading three good investment guides will surely not triple, and probably not even improve, your investment results.

The odd thing about investing—the frustrating thing —is that it is not like cooking or playing chess or much of anything else. The more cookbooks you read and pot roasts you prepare, the better the cook—within limits—you are likely to become. The more chess books you read and gambits you learn, the more opponents —within limits—you are likely to be able to outwit. But when it comes to investing: trying hard, learning strategies, knowing a lot, becoming intrigued—all these ordinarily admirable attributes may be of little help, or actually work against you. It has been amply demonstrated, as I will document further on, that a monkey with a handful of darts will do about as well at choosing stocks as most highly paid professional money managers. Show me a monkey that can make a decent veal parmesan.

If a monkey can invest as well as a professional, or nearly so, it stands to reason that you can, too. It further stands to reason that, unless you get a kick out of it, you needn't spend a great deal of time reading investment guides, especially long ones. Indeed, the chief virtue of this one (although I hope not) may be its brevity. This one is about the forest, not the trees. Because if you can find the right forest—the right overall investment outlook—you shouldn't have to worry much about the trees. Accordingly, this book will summarily dismiss investment fields that some people spend lifetimes wandering around in. For example: It is a fact that 80 percent or more of the people who play the commodities game get burned. I submit that you have now read all you need ever read of the following not-cheap books: *The Fastest Game in Town, Trading Commodity Futures* (Reinach); *Getting Rich in Commodities, Currencies, or Coins—Before or During the Next Depression* (Vichas); *Sensible Speculating in Commodities* (Angrist); *Guide to Commodity Price Forecasting* (Jiler); *Point and Figure Commodity Trading Techniques* (Zieg); *The Commodity Futures Game* (Terweles); and *Make Money in Commodity Spreads* (Kallard).

This thing about the forest and the trees—about one's degree of perspective—bears further comment, particularly as for many of us it is second nature to feel guilty if we "take the easy way out" of a given situation. If, for example, we read the flyleaf and first and last chapters of a book, to get its thrust, instead of every plodding word.

I raise this not only because it could save you many hundreds of hours stewing over investments that will do just as well unstewed, but also because it leads into the story of The Greatest Moment Of My Life.

The Greatest Moment Of My Life occurred in the Decision Analysis class at Harvard Business School. Harvard Business School uses the "case method" to impart its wisdom, which, on a practical level, means preparing three or four cases a night for the following day's classroom analysis. Typically, each case sets forth an enormous garbage dump of data, from which each student is supposed to determine how the hero or heroine of the case—inevitably an embattled division manager or company president—should ideally act. Typically, too, I could not bring myself to prepare the cases very thoroughly.

The format of the classroom discussion was that 75 of us would be seated in a semicircle with name cards in front of us, like United Nations delegates, and the professor would select without warning whomever he thought he could most thoroughly embarrass to take the first five or ten minutes of class, solo, to present his or her analysis of the case. Then everyone else could chime in for the remainder of the hour.

On one such occasion, we had been asked to prepare a case for Decision Analysis, the nub of which was: What price should the XYZ Company set for its sprockets? Not coincidentally, we had also been presented with a textbook chapter containing some elaborate arithmetic/algebraic way of determining such things. The theory behind it was simple enough—charge the price that will make you the most money—but the actual calculations, had one been of a mind to do them, were extremely time-consuming. (This was just before pocket calculators reached the market.)

The professor, a delightful but devious man, noting the conspicuous absence of densely covered yellow notepaper by my station, had the out-and-out malevolence to call on me to lead off the discussion. I should note that this occurred early in the term, before much ice had been broken and while everyone was taking life *very* seriously.

My instinct was to say, with contrition: "I'm sorry, sir, I'm not prepared"—a considerable indignity—but in a rare moment of inspiration I decided to concoct a bluff, however lame. (And here is where we get, at last, to the forest and the trees.) Said I: "Well, sir, this case obviously was meant to get us to work through the elaborate formula we were given to determine pricing, but I didn't do any of that. The case said that XYZ Company was in a very competitive industry, so I figured it couldn't charge any *more* for its sprockets than everyone else, if it wanted to sell any; and the case also said the company had all the business it could handle —so I figured there would be no point in charging *less* than everyone else, either. So I figured they should just keep charging what everybody else was charging, and I didn't do any calculations."

The professor blew his stack—but not for the reason I had expected. It seems that the whole idea of this case was to have us go round and round for 55 minutes beating each other over the head with our calculations, and *then* have the professor show us why the calculations were, in this case, irrelevant. Instead, class was dismissed twelve minutes after it began—to thunderous applause, I might add—there being nothing left to discuss.*

Now let me return to commodities.

My broker has, from time to time, tried to interest me in commodities. He trades commodities for many of his clients and—almost as proof of his faith in the product—for his own account as well. He has direct access to the head commodities man at his firm, a major New York brokerage house. He tells of clients who have churned $5,000 into $500,000.

"John," I ask, "be honest. Do *you* make money in commodities?"

"Sometimes," he says.

"Of course, *sometimes*," I say, "but overall do you make money?"

"I'm making money now. I'm up $3,200 on May [pork] bellies."

"But overall, John, if you take all the money you've made, minus your losses, commissions, and taxes, and if you divide that by the number of hours you've spent working on it and worrying about it—what have you been earning an hour?"

My broker is no fool. "I'm not going to answer that," he sort of gurgles.

It turns out that my broker has made around $5,000

*Herewith a list of all my other successes at Harvard Business School: I graduated.

before taxes in four years of commodities trading. Without a $10,000 profit once in cotton and a $5,600 profit in soybeans he would have been massacred, he says—but of course that's the whole idea in this game: a lot of little losses but a few enormous gains. He can't count the number of hours he's spent working on and worrying about commodities. He went home short sugar one Friday afternoon after it had closed up-limit (meaning that he was betting it would go down, but instead it went up so fast he didn't have time to cover his bet, and now he stood to lose even more than he put in), and spent the entire weekend, and his wife's entire weekend, worrying about it. So maybe this very smart broker, with his very smart advisors, and their very smart computer readouts, has made $2 or $3 an hour, before taxes, for his effort. And he wants *me* to play? He wants *you* to play?

If 80 percent of the people who speculate in commodities lose (and 95 percent may be a more accurate figure), the question, clearly, is how to be among the 20 percent (or 5 percent) who win. If it is not just a matter of luck, then it stands to reason that the players who have the best chance are insiders at the huge firms— Hershey, Cargill, Iowa Beef, etc.—who have people all over the world reporting to them by Telex on the slightest change in the weather, and who have a minute-to-minute feel for the market (whether it be the market for frozen orange juice, cocoa, wheat, or what-have-you). These players have, too, the backing and nerve to resist getting whipsawed out of the market when it moves against them. You are not such an insider, but those who are would be delighted to have you sit down at the table and play with them.

If, on the other hand, it *is* just luck, then you have just as good a chance as anybody else for the jackpot, and all you're doing is gambling, pure and simple, hoping to be lucky, and paying commission after commission after commission to a broker who, friend or brother-in-law though he may be, cannot bring himself to give you the right advice. He'll give you advice on October broilers, on the frost in Florida, on the technician's report he claims somehow to have seen before anybody else. Gladly. What he won't tell you—or it will cost him dearly if he does—is that you shouldn't be in the game at all.

Class dismissed.

Similarly: antique cars, wine, autographs, stamps, coins, diamonds, art. For two reasons. First, in each case you are competing against experts. If you happen already to be an expert, then you don't need, and won't pay any attention to, my advice anyway. Second, what most people fail to point out as they talk of the marvelously steady appreciation of such investments is that, while what you would have to *pay* for a given lithograph doubtless rises smartly every year, it's not so easy for the amateur to turn around and *sell* it. Galleries usually take a third to a half of the retail price as their cut—so a print that cost $100 and appreciated in five years to $200, retail, might bring you all of $100 when you went back to the gallery to sell it. Meanwhile, neither print nor wine nor diamonds nor Rolls would have been paying you dividends (other than psychic); indeed, *you* would have been paying to insure them.

As a child, I collected first-day covers (specially postmarked envelopes). Sure enough, every year they cost me more and more. Recently, discovering them in the back of a closet after a hiatus of nearly twenty years, I called a local collector I had reason to know was on the acquisition trail. (I saw his notice on the supermarket bulletin board.) Knowing you always do better if you cut out the middleman, I figured on selling them to him direct. These are beautiful first-day covers we are talking about, from the forties and fifties—hundreds of them. They had cost anywhere from 25 cents on up (although, in those days, so had a week in the country).

"How much does your collection weigh?" the buff asked, once I had suitably whetted his interest.

"How much does it *weigh?* Is your collection on a diet? It weighs a few pounds, I guess."

"I'll give you $25 for it," he said. Checking around, I found this was not an unfair price. I'm going to wait another twenty years and try again then.

Commemorative medallions (and so forth) issued ad nauseam as "instant collectors' items" by the Franklin Mint served to make the original shareholders of the Franklin Mint rich, but are much less likely to do the same for you. Their silver, gold, or platinum content is only a fraction of the selling price.

Gold itself pays no interest and costs money to insure. Moreover, it is the policy of the United States government, which still has plenty of the stuff to dump on the market, that it be a lousy investment—that it *not* be the ultimate store of value to which the world should look, nor the foundation on which national currencies should rest.

Broadway shows are fun to invest in, but you have to *pay* for your opening night seats (at least if you invest as little as I do, you do); and even if the show you back gets rave reviews, you are likely to lose all or part of what you put in. A show can linger on Broadway for a year or more, with packed houses on weekends, and not return its backers a dime.

Chain letters never work.

Things that look like cosmetics companies but are really chain letters in disguise, like Glenn Turner's Koscot Interplanetary and Holiday Magic—where the big money to be made was not in selling cosmetics, but in selling franchises to sell franchises to sell franchises (to sell cosmetics)—don't work either.

Things that involve a personal salesman who is full of enthusiasm at the prospect of making *you* rich don't work. The richer he hopes to make you, the faster you should run.

There are, in fact, very few ways to get rich quick. Fewer still that are legal. Here's one: Take $5,000 (borrow it if you have to), place it on number 22 at the nearest roulette table, and win $175,000. Don't laugh. Many complicated schemes, if they were stripped of their trappings and somehow reduced to their underlying odds, would be not much less risky. It's the trappings—the story, the pitch—that obscures the odds and persuades people to ante up the $5,000 they'd never dream of betting at roulette.

Anyway, enough of the things that won't do you much good, and on to the things that might.

CHAPTER 2

A Penny Saved Is Two Pennies Earned

A taxpayer is someone who doesn't have to take a civil service examination to work for the government.

—*Stock Trader's Almanac*

You are in a higher tax bracket than you think. At least, most people are. And this number—your tax bracket—is critical to understanding your finances.

If you earn $10,000 and pay $1,200 in federal income tax, that does *not* mean you are in the 12% tax bracket. (Any more than if you earn $100,000 and pay $12,000.) On *average* you are paying 12% of your income in federal tax, but that's not what's important. What's important in making financial decisions is how much tax you pay on the *margin*—on the last few dollars that you earn.

Because the income tax is graduated, you pay no tax on the first few dollars you earn, but a lot on the last few. That may average out to 12%; but, in the case above, if you earned another $1,000, approximately *30%* of it would go straight to the government (about $240 in federal income tax, another $60 in Social Security), and *that's* your tax bracket. Unless you happen to be subject to local income taxes as well. In New York City—admittedly the most brutal example possible—yet another $80 or so would go to state and city income taxes, so that you, the $10,000-a-year subway-riding secretary, would be in the 38% tax bracket. Congratulations.

When you add in sales taxes and property taxes, of course, the bite is even worse. But such taxes, which are not *directly* tied to what you earn, don't count in figuring your tax bracket.

Second example:

If you are single and, after all deductions and exemptions, report a taxable income of $29,000 (or if you are married and jointly report $40,000), you pay $450 of the next $1,000 you earn in federal tax. Conversely, if you gave an extra $1,000 to charity—or lost it in the stock market—you could at the same time lower your tax bill by $450, and so really be out only $550. This is what's meant by being in the 45% tax bracket.

If you live in California and report this kind of income, welcome to the 51% tax bracket. In New York City, 55.6%. The tables on pages 16–17 will give you an idea of your own tax bracket.

(Social Security tax, although included in the first example above, does not actually figure into investment decisions. Investment income does not increase the tax; deductions, like capital losses or interest expense, do not lower it. So from here on, even though you have to pay it, we can and will ignore the Social Security tax.)

To figure your bracket more accurately, just haul out last year's federal and local tax returns and calculate how much more tax you would have had to pay if you had earned an extra $1,000. Don't forget that the additional local taxes you incur would count as a deduction in figuring the federal tax—assuming that you itemize your deductions. In the second example, New York State and City taxes came to $193 on the incremental $1,000, so the amount of extra federal tax was calculated not on the full $1,000, but on the remaining $807.

The other way to figure it is to see how much in

taxes you would have *saved* if you had earned $1,000
less. This way your tax bracket may come out a few
percentage points lower, because the less you earn, the
lower your tax bracket. It doesn't make a lot of difference, but technically you would do it the first way if
you wanted to know how much of some additional income—say, dividends—you would get to keep after
taxes; and you would do it the second way if you
wanted to know how much you would save in taxes by
taking an extra deduction, such as a loss on a stock.

The idea is not to come up with some precise number, or to refigure your taxes every time the Red Cross
asks for $5, but simply to have a reasonably accurate
feel for where you stand.

Let us assume for the rest of this chapter that you
are in the 50% bracket, or not far from it. Do you
know what that means?

It means that if your boss gave you a $1,000
bonus or raise, you would get to keep $500.

It means that "time-and-a-half for overtime," since
it is all earned on the margin, is not such a posh
deal after all. After taxes, it may be no more valuable
to you—or even less so—than any other "time."

It means that 5½% interest in a savings account nets
you less than 3% (while inflation, which is *not* tax-deductible, eats away purchasing power at a much faster
rate).

It means that a 5% tax-free bond is worth as much
to you as a 10% taxable one.

It means that the first $100 of dividends you re-
ceive (or $200 if you file a joint return), being tax-
exempt, is worth twice as much to you as the first $100
($200) of interest. (So even if you've sworn off the
market, you should find some solid common or preferred stock to hold forever just to generate that much
in dividends.)

It means that a $1,000 long-term capital gain can

YOUR *APPROXIMATE* TAX BRACKET

FILING SINGLY

Net TAXABLE Income (after all deductions and exemptions):	Federal tax only*	IL, IN NJ, OH PA	RI NB VT	AL, LA MD, ME MISS MICH	AK, AR, CO, GA ID, IO, KA, KY MO, NC, NM, OK SC, UT, WV, VA	CA, DC HW, MA MT, ND OR, WI	NY MINN DEL	NY City
$ 2–4,000	16%	18%	19%	18%	17%	20%	19%	20%
$ 4–6,000	19%	21%	22%	21%	20%	23%	22%	23%
$ 6–8,000	21%	23%	24%	23%	23%	27%	25%	26%
$ 8–10,000	24%	26%	27%	27%	27%	30%	29%	31%
$10–12,000	25%	27%	28%	28%	28%	31%	31%	33%
$12–14,000	27%	29%	30%	31%	31%	33%	33%	35%
$14–16,000	29%	31%	32%	33%	33%	36%	35%	37%
$16–18,000	31%	33%	34%	35%	36%	38%	38%	40%
$18–20,000	34%	36%	37%	37%	39%	41%	41%	43%
$20–22,000	36%	38%	40%	39%	40%	42%	44%	46%
$22–24,000	38%	40%	42%	41%	42%	44%	46%	48%
$24–28,000	40%	42%	44%	43%	44%	46%	48%	50%
$28–34,000	45%	47%	49%	48%	49%	51%	53%	55%
$34–40,000	50%	52%	54%	52%	53%	55%	58%	60%
$40–46,000	55%†	57%†	59%†	57%†	58%†	60%†	62%†	64%†
$46–52,000	60%†	62%†	64%†	62%†	63%†	64%†	66%†	68%†
* * *								
$102,000+	70%†	71%†	73%†	72%†	72%†	73%†	75%†	76%†

FILING JOINTLY

$ 3–6,000	16%	18%	18%	18%	17%	19%	19%	20%
$ 7–11,000	19%	21%	22%	22%	23%	25%	25%	27%
$11–15,000	22%	24%	25%	26%	27%	29%	29%	31%
$15–19,000	25%	27%	28%	29%	30%	33%	33%	35%
$19–23,000	28%	30%	31%	32%	33%	35%	36%	38%
$23–27,000	32%	34%	35%	36%	37%	39%	41%	43%
$27–31,000	36%	38%	40%	40%	41%	43%	46%	48%
$31–35,000	39%	41%	43%	42%	43%	46%	48%	50%
$35–39,000	42%	44%	46%	45%	46%	48%	51%	53%
$39–43,000	45%	47%	49%	48%	49%	51%	53%	55%
$43–47,000	48%	50%	52%	51%	52%	53%	56%	58%
$47–55,000	50%	52%	54%	53%	54%	56%	56%	58%
$55–67,000	53%†	55%†	57%†	55%	56%	58%	58%	60%
$67–79,000	55%†	57%†	59%†	57%†	58%	60%	60%†	62%†
$79–91,000	58%†	60%†	62%†	60%†	61%†	63%†	64%†	66%†
$91–103,000	60%†	62%†	64%†	62%†	63%†	64%†	66%†	68%†
* * *								
$203,000+	70%†	71%†	73%†	72%†	72%†	73%†	75%†	76%†

NOTE: These figures are rough approximations only. The tax rates of states grouped together are similar, but by no means identical. Also, tax rates change.

This table does not include Social Security tax, because investment decisions do not raise or lower it. To include Social Security payments in your calculations, simply add 6% to all of the figures above for 8% if self-employed, up to the current (1979) ceiling of $22,900 per wage earner. Thus a self-employed New York City wallpaper hanger who would have earned $18,000 but chose to work weekends to earn an extra $1,000 would pay, in all, approximately 51% of that extra $1,000 in income and Social Security taxes (if filing singly)—assuming he reported all his income.

*Florida, Nevada, South Dakota, Texas, Washington, and Wyoming had no state income tax as of this writing. Connecticut taxed only capital gains; New Hampshire taxed only dividends and interest (other than from savings accounts) beyond the first $600 per spouse; and Tennessee taxed interest and dividends only (at 6%).

†"Earned" income is subject to a 50% maximum federal tax. Investment income, presently, is not.

be worth $250 more to you than a $1,000 short-term gain. And that taking a loss while it is still short-term can save twice as much in taxes as taking a long-term loss.

It means, above all, that a penny saved—not spent —is *two* pennies earned.

Consider: If you were planning to eat out tomorrow night, as you do every Thursday night, for around $30 with the tip, but you ate at home instead for $5, you saved $25. You have $25 more in the bank than you otherwise would have had. To *earn* an extra $25 for your bank account, you would actually have to earn $50: half for you, half for the tax men.

So if you want to pile up a little nest egg, or a big one, the first thing you might consider—even though you've doubtless considered it before—is spending less, rather than earning more. Which is what this chapter's about. If you're in the 50% tax bracket, it's twice as effective—and often easier.

If you purchased a car that averaged 30 miles to the gallon instead of 15 . . . and if an average gallon of gas over the next few years costs a buck, as it well may . . . then after having driven 50,000 miles you would have saved $1,666, cash, on gas alone, which, in the 50% tax bracket, would be like having *earned* $3,333. Or like having an extra $15,000 working for you for four years in a 5½% savings account.

What's more, the cars that get the best gas mileage tend also to cost the least. This despite the fact that in terms of the most important feature by far—getting you where you're going—they are identical to the higher-priced models. By buying an "economy car" you save substantially on the purchase price; substantially on your insurance bill (the less expensive the car, the lower the theft and collision premiums); substantially on gas; substantially on maintenance; and substantially on interest (if you finance the purchase). In all, the financial decision to be "automotively frugal"—while it is a decision you have every right not to make—could mean as much to you as having $30,000 or $40,000 extra working for you in a savings account.

Charles Revson, the late cosmetics tycoon, ordered his Cepacol by the case. By so doing, although it was the furthest thing from his mind, he did better investment-wise than he ever did in the stock market. In the stock market, with his Revlon-made fortune, Revson perennially blew tens of thousands of dollars on one or another speculation. But on Cepacol he was making 10, maybe 20 or even 30% a year, after tax.

He made it two ways: the discount he got for buying the super-economy size, in bulk; and the discount he got, in effect, by beating inflation. He got a year's worth, or two, at last year's price. If he had kept the money he spent on Cepacol in a savings account at 5½%—for him, 2½% after tax—and taken it out bit by bit to buy Cepacol in the one-at-a-time 59-cent size, where would he have been? This way, he saved maybe 30%, tax-free.

The lesson is clear, even if you are one of those people with naturally pleasant breath.

Buying a case of wine at a 10% discount ties up, say, $30 . . . but you earn $3 tax-free by doing so. If that's just three months' worth of wine for your family, over the course of the year you will save $12 by keeping $30 tied up—an annual return of 40%! Tax-free.

The point is not to make $3 on a case of wine, but to do as much of your buying this way as is practical. In the aggregate, it might tie up an extra $1,000. But between beating inflation by buying now and buying in bulk when items are on sale (or getting a by-the-case discount), you could easily be earning 20, or even 40%, on that $1,000—tax-free. It's not enough to make you rich, but neither is $1,000 in a savings bank.

This is the chicken-hearted way to play commodities, guaranteed safe for all but compulsive eaters. Forget pork bellies on 10% margin and all those other near-surefire ways to get fried. I am "long," as of this writing, a case of Campbell's soup, fourteen boxes of private-label tissue paper, four giant-sized tubes of Ultra-Brite toothpaste (bought at distress prices), several kegs of Heinz catsup, and much more. I am "short" coffee, because I expect the price to turn eventually. I was "short" sugar, too, during the 1975 insanity, which is to say I wouldn't buy any. I just ate down my inventory. Wholesale sugar prices have since fallen back down from 64 to 9 cents and I'm "long" a few pounds.

Where to put this mountainous investment? Besides the obvious, like a pantry or basement, if you have such spacious luxuries, you might also consider building your hoard under a bed or table, with a bedspread or tablecloth over the top. I know this is absurd, but I'll bet you can fit thirty cases of economy-sized tuna under just one table. Or make it a bench and put a board over it, with a cushion. Water jugs, bouillon cubes, a can opener (don't forget that!)—plan your portfolio, which doubles as a disaster hoard, and buy it on sale, in bulk. (If you're hoarding tuna, you've obviously got to hoard mayonnaise, too.)

This idea of a disaster hoard, by the way, is not such a foolish one. Nor is it "gloom and doom." Disasters *do* occur—floods, earthquakes, power outages, blizzards, civil disorder . . . and it does make sense for every household to accumulate—now, when there's no need to, at sale prices—enough nonperishables to last a while. A gallon of peanut butter. A case of tuna. A case of canned fruit. Several gallons of water and juices. Such a modest stockpiling protects not just individuals, but would seem to be in the social interest as well (unlike hoarding gold, which is anti-social). Just as the nation is stronger if there are strategic stockpiles, so is the social fabric a little less susceptible to disruption or panic if everyone has an added layer of security. Odd words, I know, in tranquil times—but harmless ones, at worst.

Don't tell me about botulism, either—out of 775 billion cans of food sold between 1920 and 1975, only three produced fatal cases of botulism. Canned food lasts years. The only cans to avoid are those that are actually leaking, or that have bulged out at the ends. In any case, if you rotate your cases of food and drink, the way you used to rotate the sheets on your bed in camp—top to bottom, bottom to laundry, fresh one on top—you'll never let anything get too far out of date.

If this sort of investment takes up storage space, it also takes less effort: fewer trips to the store. And you are much less likely to run out of things. I don't think there was a day in Charles Revson's life that his breath did not smell medicine-fresh.

Now here are a few more conventional ways to save money:

● The best way to earn 18% on your money, risk-free, is by not going into hock to a department store or bank credit card. That's what most of them charge —1½% a month. Particularly if you do not itemize your deductions, and so cannot get Uncle Sam to bear some of that interest expense, it is folly to pay such rates if you can possibly avoid it. Yet many people keep money in a savings account, earning 5½%— which might be only 3% after taxes—at the same time as they are paying 18% to buy on time.

Granted, there is something to be said for disciplining yourself not to touch your savings—that money is sacred, a last resort, and so on—and it's hard to put a dollar value on that discipline. But 18%?

● Similarly, you can "earn" upwards of 10%, completely risk-free, by not financing your car. This is particularly compelling if you do not itemize your deductions and hence cannot lay off part of the finance charge on the government. Why pay 10½% on a $4,000 loan when you have $4,000 sitting in savings accounts or bonds earning 7½ or 9% *taxable* interest?

(Nonetheless, when you go to buy a car, ask enough questions about financing—what the monthly payments would work out to, etc.—so that the salesman assumes you will. Financing, every bit as much as air-conditioning or a vinyl sunroof, is a high-margin option for the dealer, and he may be able to find an extra $50 or $100 for you in the deal he makes. Only when the deal is firm and he is committed to the price should you pull out your checkbook. He's got his negotiating ploys; why shouldn't you have yours?)

● When buying auto or homeowner's insurance, "self-insure" by taking as much of the risk yourself as you can afford. You do this by choosing the highest possible "deductible" category. In the case of auto collision insurance, this usually means paying the first $250 of damage yourself, instead of $50. Unless you are a dreadfully unskilled or unlucky motorist, your savings in premiums will more than cover the extra money you might have to pay out in accidents. This is especially true because even people who are fully insured hesitate to hit their insurance companies for small claims, knowing that if they do their rates may well go up or their policies be canceled when they come up for renewal. Why pay for coverage you may not even use?

Collision insurance offered by one company on a 1977 Chevrolet (in Rye, New York) costs $164 a year for $50-deductible coverage—but only $83.20 for $250-deductible. The $80 difference is yours every year—tax-free—for shouldering the extra $200 risk. And *should* you have an accident and have to pay that extra $200, most of it would be tax-deductible under current tax law as a "casualty loss." So you wouldn't be out an extra $200, after all: tax savings would absorb part of the loss.*

● When buying life insurance, *shop around*. Premiums vary by 50% and more for equivalent coverage. Indeed, says an FTC spokesman, "Cost variations of over 100% for essentially identical coverage are not uncommon."

There are two basic kinds of life insurance: "term" and "whole" (which is also called "straight" or "ordinary"). With term insurance all you pay for—and get—is protection. If you die, they pay. With whole life you are buying a savings plan as well. Your policy accumulates "cash values," also known as "living benefits." It is not a very good savings plan, except to the extent that it disciplines you to put away money you would otherwise have squandered. If you can provide your own discipline, you will generally do better.

Insurance salesmen are very eager to sell whole life policies because their commissions on these are so much higher than on term policies. (And that, in turn, is because the insurance company profits are higher.) *Don't buy!* You would be wiser to buy "decreasing renewable term" insurance and do your saving separately. With a renewable policy you avoid having to take a physical each time you renew and can thus be assured of continuing coverage even if your health deteriorates. Decreasing renewable allows you to renew every five years, but for less each time. The sense here is that, with

---

*If you claim such a deduction, be sure to attach copies of the police accident report; repair bills; and the deductible clause of your insurance policy. Supplying as much documentation as possible helps to satisfy IRS suspicion and head off an audit.

time, the children will have grown up, mortgages will finally have been paid off, other assets will have been accumulated, and the surviving spouse will have fewer years left during which the insurance proceeds would be needed.

The most economical insurance policies are generally the group policies arranged for by an employer or association. Beyond that, the first place to look is the local savings bank—if you are lucky enough to live or work in one of the states that offer Savings Bank Life Insurance.* SBLI, although there is a ceiling on how much you can buy, is the best deal going, largely because you are not paying to support an army of salesmen, their Oldsmobiles, district managers, and golf club memberships. Savings banks that offer SBLI have competent salaried people who can advise you. And savings banks do offer term insurance as well as whole.

Here is how widely rates can vary for equivalent coverage:*

Company	Interest-adjusted Cost Index
Company A	$ 85.60
Company B	95.20
Company C	109.00
Company D	114.20
Company E	123.40
SBLI	53.60

*Based on equivalent whole life policies being offered by the five largest life insurance companies and SBLI in New York in 1976.

For an analysis of how much life insurance you should carry, see the appendix "How Much Life Insurance Do You Need?"

---

*At this writing: New York, Massachusetts, and Connecticut. In other states, most recently California, the insurance lobby has managed to squelch the introduction of SBLI. However, if you have a *relative* living or working in one of those states, he or she may be able to apply for you, even though you, the insured, live elsewhere.

● If you have substantial whole life policies already, it may pay you handsomely to switch them: either into term policies, or even into different whole life policies.

It's true that cashing in a whole life insurance policy prematurely, for its "surrender value," is not something one does casually. After all, in the early years of the policy much of your premiums are going to pay off sales commissions and company overhead—your surrender value will be disappointingly small.

But things have changed dramatically for insurance companies—and, in turn, for insurance buyers—because of inflation. The inflation of the last several years has greatly increased the rate of return insurance companies earn on their investments; and that has allowed them to provide equivalent amounts of coverage at much lower rates than they used to.

If your whole life policy is of the "participating" variety, then the insurance company may have been passing some of the benefits of higher interest rates on to you in the form of higher dividends. But if your whole life policy does not pay dividends, and if you signed up for it more than ten years ago, then you should definitely find out what you would save in premiums by cashing in your policy and buying a new one.

Whole life insurance is like term insurance plus a savings account. So all I am really saying is—Hey! Savings banks aren't paying just 3% on your money, like they used to—now they're paying much more! Why keep your money in a 3% account whose rate was fixed many years ago?

To find out whether you would save hundreds of dollars a year in premiums by switching your current whole life contract to a new one—or to term insurance—invite two or three competing life insurance salesmen to present you with analyses.

● When renting a car or truck, never sign up for the optional insurance (usually $2 or so a day extra)—

except, perhaps, on days when the roads are extremely hazardous. Even without paying this charge you are only liable for a maximum of $250 in most cases . . . a risk you can probably afford to take. The rental agencies are not offering this coverage as a favor to you—it's one of the most profitable parts of their business. Keep the profit for yourself.

● Likewise, service contracts on appliances. Companies wouldn't offer these contracts if the odds weren't with them. On average, you do better taking the risk yourself.

● A solar water heater that costs $1,000 to install but saves $200 a year on your utility bill is like an investment that returns 20% tax-free.

● Simple insulation may be the best "investment" you can make, returning as much as 50% or more, tax-free, in annual savings on heating and cooling. Why put $2,000 into the stock of some utility and earn $150 in annual taxable dividends if you can put the same money (or less) into insulation and save $150 or more, tax-free, on your utility bill? (Check also the federal tax credits that may be available to encourage such energy-saving investment.)

● A one-minute call to the Coast (East or West) can cost as much as $3.55 or as little as 22 cents—take your pick. Never call person-to-person, or with the help of an operator (as with credit card calls), if you can possibly help it. Direct-dialing is much less expensive, particularly on weekends and after eleven at night. If you have kids away at school, ask them *not* to call collect. That adds nearly $1.50 to the cost of a typical station-to-station call. They should either signal you to call them or call you direct and allow you to reimburse them later. (Trivial? With two kids calling weekly over four years of college, the savings comes to nearly $500.)

● Fly night coach. You avoid the rush hours to and

from the airport and are less likely to be delayed or crowded. Many "night flights" leave as early as nine o'clock, and you save 20% or more, tax-free.

● Write away for the Best Products, Sears, and Spiegel catalogs and keep them on your reference shelf. (Best Products, Box 26303, Richmond, VA 23260—name brands at hefty discounts and fast service—a one-time $1 charge to be put on their mailing list; Sears, Sears Tower, Chicago, IL 60684; Spiegel, Box 8282, Philadelphia, PA 19170.) When you need to buy something, check the catalogs first. If nothing else, this will give you a better idea of the kind of bargain you are getting (or not getting) down the street. Catalog shopping can be convenient and sometimes cheap—in part because catalog houses must set their prices far in advance and are less able to raise them month by month with inflation.

● Avoid buying lottery tickets with your spare dollar at the checkout counter. The state lotteries pay out barely 50 cents in prizes for every dollar they take in; but since all the big prizes are heavily taxed, the odds are even worse. Heads you win 30 cents, tails you lose $1.

● Discount gas, most experts agree, is just as good as lavishly advertised gas.

● You will use appreciably less of it if you have radial tires and if you drive smoothly. Rapid accelerations are murder on gas mileage; unnecessary braking is a means of converting kinetic energy, through friction, to useless heat. "Good driving habits" and a well tuned engine can save as much as a third of a family's gasoline bill.

● Quit smoking. There's $300 or $400 a year after tax right there . . . although by adding five or ten years to your probable life span you will greatly increase the cost of your retirement. On second thought, smoke all you want.

● Have your doctor write prescriptions for "generic" drugs, not brand-name drugs. The only difference is the price—often a difference of 200 or 300%.

● Synthetic vitamins are chemically identical to natural ones and cost much less. There is no persuasive evidence that vitamins in excess of normal daily requirements do any good anyway.

● Private-label merchandise is often made on exactly the same production line, with the same ingredients, as the more expensive advertised brands. Aspirin is aspirin, no matter how elaborate the commercials get.* It is a sad fact of American consumer patterns that poor people, in particular, avoid private-label brands, despite the potential savings, so persuasive is national advertising. For example, private-label shaving cream, menthol or plain, is occasionally on sale at 49 cents. Believe me, it works just as well as the name brands on the next shelf that sell for $1.59.

Granted, not all private-label merchandise is as good as its name-brand competition. None of it, presumably, is better. But is it really worth 80% more to you to sneeze into a genuine Kleenex-brand "kleenex"?

Consumer Reports is devastating in comparing such brands as Bayer, Bufferin, Anacin, and Excedrin with plain 29¢-a-jar private-label aspirin. The difference is almost entirely in price, with here and there some caffeine or a trace of antacid or an aspirinlike analgesic thrown in.

	Saving this much annually by shopping, driving, phoning, flying, financing, etc., more efficiently . . .				
If you are in this tax bracket:	$250	$500	$750	$1,000	$1,500
	. . . is as good as having this much earning 5½% taxable interest for you in a savings account:				
10%	$5,051	$10,101	$15,152	$20,202	$30,303
20%	$5,682	$11,364	$17,046	$22,728	$34,092
30%	$6,493	$12,987	$19,480	$25,973	$38,961
40%	$7,576	$15,152	$22,727	$30,303	$45,454
50%	$9,091	$18,182	$27,273	$36,364	$54,545
60%	$11,363	$22,727	$34,091	$45,454	$68,182

CHAPTER 3

The Case for Cowardice

> This broker calls his customer for four straight
> years and each year puts him into some dreadful
> stock that drops right through the floor. The fifth
> year, the customer calls the broker and says,
> "Look: I don't know about all these stocks we've
> been buying—I think maybe I'd be better off in
> bonds."
>
> "Yeah, sure," says the broker, "but what do I know
> about bonds?"
>
> —Old joke

Money makes money. Put $10,000 into a savings cer-
tificate at 8% and watch it grow. In a year, without
lifting a finger or losing a minute of sleep, you will
have—presto!—maybe $9,900 of buying power left.
The exact damage depends on your tax bracket and
the inflation rate. Those ads that show how, if you're
patient, after 75 years your $2,000 will grow into
$877,499, or whatever, are deceptive. In the 75th
year, for example, when your pile would supposedly
grow by $68,371, you would have something like
$30,000 in taxes to pay on it. Where is that money
supposed to come from? After taxes, the appreciation
is far, far less dramatic (unless—see Chapter 4—you
qualify to set up a tax-deferred retirement plan).
What's more, there is no guarantee that the 8% long-
term savings certificates commonly available in 1978

will be available for 75 years. Interest rates could go down.*

Savings accounts are for the chicken-hearted. They are no way to get rich. But if you think I'm launching into a pitch for finding "the next Xerox" or for speculating in Canadian mining shares, you are wrong. I respect the right to be chicken-hearted. Well, if the truth be known, I am rather chicken-hearted myself. Much of my own money is stashed away (tax-deferred) in the Lincoln Savings Bank. It's not that I have more than occasional doubts about the long-term viability of the American economy—listen, *I* was bullish on America even before Merrill Lynch started advertising! *I* was bullish on America back in 1968 and 1969, when the market started to fall apart! It's just that I don't want to lose too much money.

With prices rising like yeast, it is tempting to abandon one's conservative ways and look for an investment vehicle that will rise in value at least as fast. But the chicken-hearted way to beat inflation is to *eat* at McDonald's, not invest in it.

Really, the challenge of chicken-hearted investing isn't deciding where to put your money, but resisting the temptation to put it elsewhere. *Face it: sure things are boring*. Treasury bills have terribly predictable plots that make lousy cocktail party conversation (even if they do have some redeeming snob appeal), and they won't make you rich. If the United States Treasurer really wanted to sell those bills, she would issue them at slightly lower interest rates—and put the difference into a kitty for which there would be a daily drawing. The United States Lottery. That would give Treasury bill buyers something to check in the paper

---

*In the 75-year example above I assumed interest would be compounded daily, which raises the effective annual interest rate from 8 to 8.45%— and the final sum by no less than $235,000. Such is the power of compound interest. (See the appendix "Fun with Compound Interest.")

every day and a chance—however thin—to strike it rich.

Once in a long while you do find a sure thing with an outsized payoff, but it is very rare. The only time I was ever so fortunate was years ago, with a stock called Nation-Wide Nursing Centers. Of course, under normal circumstances nursing home stocks are not fare for the chicken-hearted. But this was one of those rare sure things. Through some remarkable good luck, on a day when this stock was selling for $22 a share over-the-counter—that was the price you would have paid—*I* was able to snag 500 shares at just $8 each, "under-the-counter." The only hitch was that the shares were "unregistered," which meant I couldn't sell them for a while. It was a virtual gift of $7,000, which was hard enough to believe, let alone turn down.

Ordinarily, however, there is no such thing as a financial bargain. The financial markets are too large and efficient for that. By and large, you get what you pay for. Or, if you try to get more, you generally get what's coming to you. I was told I would have to hold my nursing home stock for three months, when it would almost surely be bought out by a merger-mad steel company at $40 a share. The head of research for one of Wall Street's most prestigious firms was in the deal for 4,000 shares, so I knew this was on the up and up.

The stock is now zero, and I am still expecting to hear from that steel company any day.

There are two kinds of money in the world, debt and equity. Debt is an IOU; equity is a piece of the action. Debt is bonds or bills or notes or savings accounts—anything where you *lend* your money, whether to the U.S. government, a local government, a savings bank, a corporation—whomever. (Yes, when you deposit money in a savings bank, you are actually lending the bank money. The bank is in your debt and must pay you interest. You have taken their IOU in exchange for your cash.) Equity is where you *invest* your money, with no promise that your investment will be recouped, but with the reasonable assurance that as the company prospereth or falleth into decline, so shall you prosper or fall.

Until you have $5,000 or $10,000 in a savings account, unless you are so wealthy you don't have to worry about the contingencies of everyday living, like losing your job, you are crazy even to consider making riskier investments. Or more sophisticated ones. Relax: You are doing just the right thing. You are missing no great opportunities. You are *not* a sap. There is a time and a place for everything, and when cocktail party conversation turns to "investments," or "the market," I suggest the time has come for you to be smug. Let the others do what they do, say what they say— you are above it. They may gamble, they may speculate, they may talk of doubling their money (and not mention halving it); you are smug. (See pages 174–5 for a list of smug rejoinders and harmless financial one-liners to keep up your end of the conversation.)

The television campaign the savings bank people have run from time to time about commercial banks being for businesses, while savings banks are for people—"and I'm a people"—is so silly as not to bear discussion. But the other one you may have seen, which shows a man recounting his sad history of investment failures, and then has him brightening to say that now his money is in a savings bank—he's "found a better way"—that one may be equally simpleminded, but it's really not bad advice. The first several thousand dollars of anybody's money (aside from equity in a home) should be in a savings bank. And for many people, that's *all* their money.

It's true that even for small amounts of money there

are "fixed-income securities," such as bonds, that are safe and may pay a little better than a savings certificate. But there is also the question of time. How much is yours worth?

The extra 1% you might earn on $5,000 comes to $50 a year. Less taxes, maybe $30. (And the commission on buying five $1,000 bonds may be $25.) Now you have bonds; and now when you go to sell them, it's more trouble than going to your corner savings bank (and you pay another $25 commission); and—*who cares? How much money are we talking about?*

The books that really get me are the ones they advertise that promise to tell you "How to Make Up to 13½% or More on Your Savings—All Fully Insured!" The ads run on to say how upset the savings banks are about this book, but there's nothing they can do, and the interest you earn can be even more than 13½%, etc., etc. And when you send for the book—can you really have expected differently? —you find that to earn these astounding rates of interest you have to spend most of your waking life transferring money with split-second precision from one bank on a Friday afternoon to another that handles its accounting a different way, and back and forth and around—*and even then you are only earning this rate a few days out of the year*. You do *not* earn 13% annually. Most of the time you earn just 5½%, or whatever is the going rate; *sometimes* you jigger it so you can earn at a 13% annual rate over a long weekend. That sort of thing. (In the meantime, you could have been earning 8% or so continuously, in a long-term savings account.) And for those extra dimes and nickels over the weekend—*who cares?*

One such book was advertised a few years ago— full-page ads in reputable magazines, for months—as being available only by mail, at $8.98. In fact, a 95-

cent paperback edition was available in stores while the ad was running. The author told me: "After reading the huckster's copy on my book, you wonder whether they're the same books! The way they're advertised—I know if I bought one, I'd be steaming mad." Nonetheless, he wrote at least one more such book for the same publisher.

The one gimmick you should know about the savings bank game, if you can call it that, is that it generally pays to put at least some of your money into a long-term account at the highest possible interest. (Forget those accounts that require 90 days' notice of withdrawal in return for giving you an extra ¼% interest—that's just a nuisance.) Tying up your money for several years may help provide some self-discipline along with the substantially higher interest. And if you *do* have to withdraw your savings, the penalty is not particularly severe: the interest is recalculated to what it would have been at the short-term rate, and you forfeit three months' worth. Since the short-term rate is all you would have been getting anyway, you stand to lose very little. To facilitate matters, I suggest splitting your funds up into as many certificates as possible. That is, if $1,000 is the minimum requirement but you have $4,000, you could have the bank issue you four separate long-term certificates. That way it could be easier to cash one in early without disturbing the rest of your money.

As for the checking accounts that pay interest, or the savings accounts against which you can write checks (which amounts to the same thing), naturally it is better to draw interest than to leave money sitting idle. If you live in a state that does not yet allow such interest-bearing checking accounts, you can easily set up a bank-by-mail account at a bank in a state that does (such as the large New York savings banks or First National Bank of Boston). However, check the service charges and minimum balance requirements before signing up. And keep perspective: if your bank balance averages $500, switching to an interest-bearing account will mean at most $25 or $30 a year in added interest— $15 after tax. Not worth a great deal of effort pursuing.

Finally there is the important new wrinkle that was added in mid-1978: The special six-month savings certificates most savings banks offer, in units of $10,000, pay a rate of interest equal to the current Treasury bill rate plus ¼%—compounded daily. (Thus, when Treasuries were yielding 7.16%, these certificates were paying 7.41%, which, because of daily compounding, was an effective rate of 7.8%.)

For those who can afford them, these certificates are a very good deal. They offer convenience, a short maturity, and, when interest rates are high, a generous return.

If, then, you have $10,000 or less, you know what to do with it. You've probably already done it: It's in a savings bank. If this book hasn't made a dime for you, at least it's confirmed your good sense. And you can always start reading again when your fortunes swell. (Well, do read the next chapter, because you may be able to salt away and compound your savings tax-free.)

For those who have got enough money to make an extra point or two of interest worth worrying over, there are three things that will determine what you can get for it, three things the financial markets reward: volume, patience, and risk. To each of the three, the same refrain dolefully applies: the rich get richer.

Volume. As with any product, financial or otherwise, if you buy in quantity, you get discount prices. To buy and sell 50 shares of AT&T costs the little guy roughly

4% in commissions, which takes some of the bloom off AT&T's 6% dividend. To buy and sell 5,000 shares costs Big Money less than a half a percent. Similarly, the typical $15 service charge on a purchase of $10,000 90-day Treasury bills cuts the effective annual interest rate by .6%. There is no service charge on "round lots"—multiples of $100,000.

It is well known that the odds are worst for the little guy—whether it be the dreadful odds of the state lotteries or the only slightly less dreadful odds of the nickel slot machines. The smaller the stakes, the larger the cut the house demands.

Patience. The longer you are willing to tie up your money, the higher the interest rate you will ordinarily be paid for it. (During occasional "credit crunches," short-term rates may temporarily exceed long-term rates.) One reason for this is that the future is unpredictable, so the further into it you tie up your money, the more you are being exposed to the third variable:

Risk. The more risk you take, the greater your potential reward (and the greater your chance of loss—see the graph). But how much risk—even if it is, in your opinion, a "good" risk—can you afford to take?

If I offered you 2-to-1 odds on the flip of an honest coin—heads you win $20, tails you lose $10—wouldn't you take the bet? But what if the odds were the same, only you stood to lose $1,000? Or $50,000? Wherever you draw the line is one measure of your chicken-heartedness—which is doubtless justified. There are a lot of excellent risks around that people of limited means just cannot prudently accept.

One of them may be the stock market . . . but that is another chapter. For now, what are the alternatives to savings banks for the investor who wants to take only minimal risk?

The Only Graph in This Book

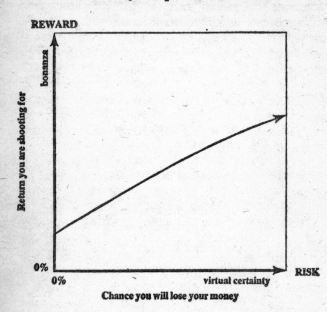

Broadly speaking, these financial "instruments," also called "debt instruments," can be divided into short- and long-term—just as your own credit card borrowings are short-term, while your mortgage seems to stretch on into eternity.

Short-term Instruments

For short-term investment with maximum safety, the most practical, convenient alternative to the local savings bank is one of the money-market mutual funds. Dreyfus Liquid Assets and Fidelity Daily Income Trust are currently the largest and best known.

The money-market funds merge your initial deposit (minimum $1,000 to $5,000, depending on the fund) with hundreds of millions of dollars more and then invest it in blue-chip short-term government and corporate obligations such as U.S. Treasury bills (denominated in $10,000s and issued with 3-, 6-, 9-, and 12-month maturities); commercial paper (denominated in $100,000s or more and issued like IOUs for short periods by major corporations); "c.d.'s" (certificates of deposit issued by banks, denominated in $100,000s or more); and soon-to-mature government agency bonds, World Bank bonds, and Treasury notes or Treasury bonds.* You are credited with your share of the interest daily and can withdraw any amount at any time. You can even arrange to write checks on your account, in the amount of $500 or more, at no charge—and your money will continue earning interest in the fund until the check actually clears. Thus a money-market fund is not unlike a checking account that pays interest, or a savings account on which you can write checks, except that the interest rate varies daily with the money market. It is perfectly legitimate for you to deposit money in one of these funds when their rate is higher than that of the savings banks, and to take it out again when their rate dips lower. You can do this as often as you like at no charge.

The funds charge no sales commission or redemption fee; they rake about ¾% off the top of the interest that they earn. But unless you are enormously wealthy, with a penchant for drudgery to boot, the time and trouble these funds save you are worth the management fee—not to mention the diversification and buying power they provide. And although they are not themselves federally insured, the securities they invest in on your behalf entail very little risk. What's more, the actual cash and securities are held in a major bank.

*The only real difference between Treasury bills, bonds, and notes is the length of time for which they are issued. Treasury bills have maturities up to 1 year; Treasury notes have maturities from 1 year to 10; Treasury bonds are issued with maturities of more than 10 years.

There may be long periods when the rates at these funds will not be worth bothering about. During a "credit crunch," however, the funds might be paying you 8%, versus the 5 or 5½% you would be getting in a daily savings account. To find out the current rate for each of the funds, and to receive their prospectuses and "descriptive brochures," simply write, or call, toll-free, 800-223-5525 for Dreyfus Liquid Assets (212-935-5700 collect if you live in New York state), 800-225-6190 for Fidelity (617-726-0650 collect in Massachusetts).

Long-term Instruments—Background

When you buy a bond you are lending money, whether to Uncle Sam, General Motors, or the City of Houston. There are three risks involved in buying a bond. The first is that you won't get paid back. The second is that you will get paid back early. The third is that, should you want to sell the bond some time before maturity (the payback date), you won't be able to get as much for it as you paid.

The first risk is a function of the creditworthiness of the borrower. If you're lending your money to the federal government, or even to most local governments and major corporations, you have little to worry about. If you're lending to an entity that is a bit touch-and-go —New York City, Lockheed, most airlines—you do have something to worry about, but you will be paid to worry.

Happily, you need not spend more than a few minutes investigating the creditworthiness of the entities whose bonds you are considering. This is done *for* you in two ways. First, every major bond is rated by two rating services, Standard & Poor's and Moody's. *Their* men in green eyeshades pore over balance sheets and tax bases and quick ratios and coverage ratios

—and reduce it all for you to schoolgrades. Triple-A (AAA) is the best. Anything with a *B* in it (Baa, for example) means "Beware"; it is *probably* OK, except this is the chapter about taking minimal risk and sleeping soundly at night, so stick to A-rated, or even double-A-rated, bonds, even though they pay a little less. (C-rated bonds are pure speculations—very serious risk, but substantial potential reward.)

Even without checking the ratings, you can tell the quality of a bond just by looking at how its yield compares with the yields of other bonds. These are reasonably "efficient" markets, and you just are not going to find one Telephone bond that is way out of line with the rest, nor a General Motors bond that pays as well as an American Motors bond. If anything, you should shy away from bonds that pay exceptional interest: there is a reason why they pay so well.

(Really, you can get just about any interest rate you want. You want 8%? Here's a General Motors bond. You want 9%? Have some Delta Airlines. Eleven percent? How about Rapid American? Thirteen percent? How about Rapid American maturing ten years later?)

If you are looking at corporate bonds, first check to see what GM and the phone company are yielding on bonds of similar maturity. You can probably afford to take a little more risk than this, and get a little higher return (for example, subsidiaries of the phone company, like New York Telephone, pay a little better than Ma Bell, but must be nearly as safe); but don't reach too far.

Also, because the world is highly uncertain, even for monoliths like the phone company, it is only prudent to diversify—even among AA-rated bonds. Don't lend *all* your money to Pacific Telephone—the earthquake, or a breakthrough in mental telepathy, could ruin you.

Yet it doesn't pay to spread your money over *too* many different bonds, because the flip side of diversification is volume. Bonds are denominated in $1,000s,* and any order for fewer than five at a time, while you can probably get it executed, is likely to cost an extra 2 or 3% or more in the spreads that bond dealers take for their trouble.

The second thing to watch out for in buying a bond is its "callability." Many bonds are issued with provisions that allow the issuer to call them in before maturity. When this happens, you get paid back—often with a small premium—but you then have to go out looking for a new place to lend your money. And since borrowers have a tendency to call their bonds in when interest rates have fallen, you may be sorry you didn't buy a noncallable bond.

The third risk in buying bonds is that you may not be able to get back what you paid when you go to sell them—even though, if you held on to maturity, you would get the full $1,000 face value of each bond.

This third risk is a function of the money market.

There is a market for money just as there is a market for everything else—coffee, plywood, lemons—and when lots of people are trying to borrow but few are willing to lend, the price—namely, interest rates—goes up. When few are trying to borrow and many are eager to lend, the price—interest rates—goes down. Simple supply and demand, plus a good dose of government intervention. (The government sets certain interest rates by fiat, which affects other interest rates; more important, the government controls the overall supply of money—which unlike coffee, plywood, or lemons does not grow on trees.)

The key to everything financial, and to nearly ev-

---

*Don't be confused by the way they are quoted—as a percentage of par ($1,000). A bond selling at 88¼—88¼% of par—costs $882.50; at 94½, $945.00; at 106⅜, $1,063.75.

erything economic, is interest rates. When the going rate for money rises, bond prices automatically (and stock prices almost as automatically) fall. When the going rate for money falls, bonds (and stocks) rise. There is nothing mysterious about this; it is simple arithmetic. If you paid $1,000 ("par," also known as "face value") for a bond that paid $50 a year interest, and then interest rates went up such that newly issued bonds were paying $70 interest, who in his right mind would buy yours for $1,000? Why would anyone take 5% interest when the going rate has risen to 7%? If, however, you offered the bond at, say, $850, you might be able to sell it (depending on how long it had to run to maturity), because the buyer would be getting $50 interest on $850—5.88%—*plus* the prospect of a $150 profit when the bond matured.

(On stock prices, interest rates have a double-barreled effect. For one thing, the higher interest rates go in the bond markets, the less attractive stock dividends look by comparison . . . so people sell stocks to buy bonds, and stock prices fall until dividends *do* look attractive. Also, high interest rates mean high costs to business and less incentive to invest, expand, employ— all the things that make the economy boom, profits flow, and stock prices climb.)

There are different interest rates for different kinds of borrowers and different kinds of loans, but they all move in rough tandem. If the rate banks charge their prime customers goes up, you can be sure the rates they charge their lesser customers will go up as well; if corporations have to pay more interest to float a bond issue, you can be sure municipalities do, too.

Interest rates, furthermore, sit on top of inflation. If inflation is running at 6% a year, lenders are going to feel awfully foolish lending their money at 5%— so they don't. As a general rule of thumb, long-term interest rates on high-quality bonds run around 3%

above lenders' expectations of long-term inflation rates.

For a bit of perspective, let alone nostalgia, see on the next page how interest rates have fluctuated since 1920. Up, mostly.

You will notice that someone who bought a 20-year 3% bond at face value ($1,000) when it was issued in 1955, entitling him to $30-a-year interest until 1975, probably began to feel regretful around the year 1957, when similar bonds were being issued at nearly 4% —$40-a-year interest. It is the same feeling one would have buying a TV set shortly before it went on sale, or shortly before a greatly improved model was released.

Had one, on the other hand, bought a 30-year AA-rated Public Service Electric and Gas bond at par ($1,000) in October 1974, when issued at 12%, as interest rates were peaking, one could have turned around and sold it for $1,200 3 years later . . . or sat smugly collecting $120 in interest on the $1,000 investment while most others were earning only $80 or so.

Clearly, if you knew which way interest rates were going, you could profit many ways. Many people therefore try to guess, and some, in any given year, guess right. Few, however, can guess right consistently, least of all you or I or the man on all-news radio. Experts disagree; and the majority view at any given time is about as likely to be wrong as the minority view. The one thing on which there is nearly unanimous agreement is the difficulty of predicting interest rates.

That notwithstanding, I pay particular attention to the opinions of Citibank,* to which most of the world is in hock anyway, so they should know; and of Ben Weberman, who currently writes a column in *Forbes* magazine, and who has been at this game a long time.

---

*Citibank publishes, free, *Monthly Economic Letter,* 399 Park Avenue, New York, N.Y. 10022.

A Table That Looks Boring
But Is Actually Most Revealing

Year	Prime Rate	Triple-A Bonds	Municipal Bonds	Savings Accounts	Home Mortgages	Inflation
1920	6.58%	6.12%	4.98%	4 %	5.75%	2.3%
1925	4.98	4.88	4.09	4	5.90	3.8
1929	6.02	4.73	4.27	4½	5.92	0
1930	3.50	4.55	4.07	4½	5.95	—6.0
1935	1.50	3.60	2.40	2½	5.26	3
1940	1.50	2.84	2.50	2	5.40	.1
1945	1.50	2.62	1.67	1½	4.70	2.3
1946	1.50	2.53	1.64	1½	4.74	18.2
1947	1.52	2.61	2.01	1½	4.80	9.0
1948	1.85	2.82	2.40	1½	4.91	2.7
1949	2.00	2.66	2.21	1½	4.93	1.8
1950	2.07	2.62	1.98	2	4.95	5.8
1951	2.56	2.86	2.00	2	4.93	5.9
1952	3.00	2.96	2.19	2½	5.03	.9
1953	3.17	3.02	2.72	2½	5.09	.6
1954	3.05	2.90	2.37	2½	5.15	— .5
1955	3.16	3.06	2.53	2¾	5.18	.4
1956	3.77	3.36	2.93	2¾	5.19	2.9
1957	4.20	3.89	3.60	3	5.42	3.0
1958	3.83	3.79	3.56	3¼	5.58	1.8
1959	4.48	4.38	3.95	3¼	5.71	1.5
1960	4.82	4.41	3.73	3½	5.85	1.5
1961	4.50	4.35	3.46	3½	5.87	.7
1962	4.50	4.33	3.18	4	5.90	1.2
1963	4.50	4.26	3.23	4	5.84	1.6
1964	4.50	4.40	3.22	4	5.78	1.2
1965	4.54	4.49	3.27	4	5.74	1.9
1966	5.62	5.13	3.82	4	6.14	3.4
1967	5.63	5.51	3.98	4	6.33	3.0
1968	6.28	6.18	4.51	4	6.83	4.7
1969	7.95	7.03	5.81	4	7.66	6.1
1970	7.91	8.04	6.50	4¼	8.27	5.5
1971	5.70	7.39	5.70	4¼	7.59	3.4
1972	5.25	7.21	5.27	4¼	7.45	3.4
1973	8.02	7.44	5.18	5	7.95	8.8
1974	10.80	8.57	6.09	5¼	8.92	12.2
1975	7.86	8.83	6.89	5¼	8.75	7.0
1976	6.83	8.44	6.64	5¼	8.90	4.8
1977	6.82	8.20	5.68	5¼	8.68	6.5
1978 est	9.5	9.0	6.1	5¼	9.6	9.5

Then I flip a coin.

Certainly rates in the fifties seemed very high by comparison to the forties—yet in the sixties rates climbed still higher. With hindsight—as of this writing, at least—it is clear that in 1974 one should have locked himself into medium-grade 30-year 11% bonds (or 7% tax-free municipals). But by the time you read this—or by the next time you do—rates could be even higher. Or spiraling inflation could shatter the value of the currency altogether, as it did in Germany post–World War I, in which case *any* long-term fixed-income security becomes worthless. On the other hand, imagine having 10% bonds five years from now if inflation and interest rates fell back to the level of the fifties.

It becomes a question not so much of which high-quality borrower you want to lend your money to—that's easy, it doesn't matter—but of how long you are willing to get tied in to a particular rate.

The first answer, as with any other financial question, is to diversify. It makes little sense to put all your money into bonds of one maturity—say, 20-year bonds—any more than it makes sense to put all your money into one bond.

The second answer is that you are not an insurance company—founded in 1734 and not likely to founder much before 2234 (merge, maybe; founder, no)—and so, not having that kind of endless inflow of big dollars, nor institutional immortality, you should probably not tie up too much of your money in 30-year bonds. (You can always sell the bonds, of course, but if interest rates rise, you will sell at a loss.)

On the other hand, equity investments over the last 50 years haven't averaged out to return much more than 9% (dividends plus appreciation), so if the opportunity arises to lock in a sure 9% for twenty or thirty years, with none of the bother or risk or brokerage commissions of choosing stocks—it will be hard to go wrong.

We have become increasingly aware in this country that inflation of much more than 2% or 3%—or certainly 5%—is murderous. It drives up interest rates, eats away at profits, lowers living standards, stifles the incentive to invest, worsens unemployment. Runaway "double-digit" inflation is the economic equivalent of nuclear disaster, a thing that must be avoided at all costs—or so most economists and politicians believe —if the economic order is to survive. As a result, one expects a great deal of effort and energy to be applied at the highest levels to keep interest rates from rising much above their peaks of 1974.

This was not nearly so much the case in the fifties and early sixties, when the rise in inflation and interest rates, while unwelcome, was not widely perceived to threaten the foundations of the society. Inflation of 2% and long-term interest rates of 5% are apparently well within the system's tolerance, but double-digit inflation is something else again entirely. The difference can be sensed from the compound-interest tables, which grow fairly leisurely at 2 or 4%, but alarmingly at 8% and explosively at 12%. In 30 years, $1 grows to $3.24 at 4% interest—and shrinks in buying power to 54 cents at 2% inflation, which may be more to the point. But at 12%, the dollar grows not three times as fast, but nine times as fast—to $29.96 in 30 years. And at 12% inflation it shrinks not to 54 cents but to 2 cents.

The prospect of $1 shrinking in value to 2 cents in 30 years (or to 46 cents in just 6 years) is not one that encourages people or companies to invest their money in long-term projects. And without such investments, the productive machine eventually grinds to a halt. Capitalism fails.

Knowing this, union leaders, businessmen, bankers,

and politicians alike all are anxious to keep inflation and interest rates low enough, at least, to allow the system to survive. Hence, long-term interest rates are not likely to keep climbing in the eighties and nineties as they have, fairly steadily, since the thirties. It's hard to see how they could without the system's collapsing altogether. That is, of course, a possibility, but in that case not many other investments would fare much better than 8 or 10% bonds, anyway.

So much for background.

Long-term Instruments—Specifics

Savings bank **savings certificates,** currently yielding as much as 8.45%, are the most convenient way to earn a better-than-plain-vanilla return on your money, and they involve no risk. Savings accounts are federally insured at most banks up to $40,000. However, the certificates are illiquid. You can't sell them to someone else. And you forfeit a good deal of the interest if you withdraw early (see page 35).

U.S. savings bonds make nice gifts for a baby, but are a poor investment and are equally illiquid. You can do better in other bonds, or in a long-term savings certificate. They do offer tax advantages—they are exempt from state and local taxes, and you don't have to pay tax on the interest until you cash them in—but if you need tax advantages, you should probably be in municipal bonds instead.

Municipal bonds. There are two kinds of bonds: most of them, which are taxable; and municipals, which are not. The interest on bonds issued by state and local governments, county sewage authorities, and the like is federal income tax–free. You don't even have to report it. In most cases, it is also exempt from local taxes of the same region. New York City bonds, for example, are exempt from New York State and New York City income tax (but not from California income tax—California's bonds are). The table on page 50 compares the value of tax-free interest with taxable interest. The higher your marginal tax bracket, the more sense it makes for you to look for tax-free bonds, even though in absolute dollars they pay less than taxable bonds of comparable risk and maturity.

(In addition to its "current yield," a bond selling for less than its $1,000 "face value" will, at maturity, pay off the full $1,000, providing you with an additional profit. That profit, if you've held for a year or more, *is* taxed, but as a long-term capital gain.*)

It is possible that some day the tax-free status of municipals will be revoked—although I doubt it. That would just force local governments to pay higher rates for the money they borrow, which in turn would mean raising local taxes (or else seeking a federal subsidy, as has been proposed). But even if municipals did lose their tax exemption, it is almost inconceivable that the law would affect those bonds that had already been issued. More likely, the new law would affect only bonds issued thereafter. In which case, if anything, old municipals would likely *rise* in value, because there would be a limited and gradually shrinking pool of such bonds.

Caution: I know what you are thinking. Why not borrow money at 10%, which in the 50% tax bracket comes to only 5% after taxes, and use it to buy municipals that yield 6% tax-free? Make a profit without putting up a dime! It's a great idea, only Uncle Sam has thought of it, too. The IRS will disallow interest deduc-

---

*A capital gain results when you sell something—be it a stock, a bond, or gold coins—at a profit. If you have owned it less than a year, the profit is called a short-term capital gain, and is taxed just as if it were regular income. If you have owned it more than a year, it is a long-term capital gain and, under current law, only half of it is taxed.

	A tax-free bond that yields . . .			
	4.0%	5.0%	6.0%	7.0%
If your marginal tax bracket * is	. . . is as good, after-tax, as a taxable investment that yields:			
0	4.0%	5.0%	6.0%	7.0%
10%	4.4%	5.5%	6.7%	7.8%
20%	5.0%	6.3%	7.5%	8.8%
25%	5.3%	6.7%	8.0%	9.3%
30%	5.7%	7.1%	8.6%	10.0%
35%	6.2%	7.7%	9.2%	10.8%
40%	6.7%	8.3%	10.0%	11.7%
45%	7.3%	9.1%	10.9%	12.7%
50%	8.0%	10.0%	12.0%	14.0%
55%	8.9%	11.2%	13.3%	15.6%
60% ‡	10.0%	12.5%	15.0%	17.5%

*See Chapter 2. If the bond you are considering is not exempt from your local income tax, then it is only your marginal federal income tax bracket that is relevant here.

‡There are situations in which you can be in an even higher tax bracket. But if you are, you must already have a tax advisor working to get you out of it, and I wish you and your family, and the chauffeur and servants, well.

tions if in its view the interest was incurred to obtain funds to buy tax-free bonds.

Government bonds, issued by the U.S. government and its agencies, are both liquid and safe, except that if you want to sell them before they mature, and if interest rates have risen in the meantime, you will suffer a loss. For a listing of government bonds, when they mature, and what they are yielding, look in the back pages of the *Wall Street Journal*. At first the numbers and abbreviations may put you off, but the fog will clear. For each category of government or government agency bonds there will be listed a range of maturities, from bonds that mature this year to some that don't mature until the next century. You will notice that in each case—except during a credit crunch"—the "yield" rises gradually with the maturity. Patience is rewarded.

Government bonds, unlike municipals, are fully taxable by the federal government but *not* subject to state or municipal taxes. They may be purchased through your commercial banker or your broker, although neither will be thrilled with the business: the commissions they charge on this kind of transaction are very low.

The real problem with government bonds is that the federal government is considered such a good risk—the bonds are *so* safe—they don't pay very good interest.

Take a chance. Lend your money to General Motors or AT&T and earn higher interest. (Unless you are in a high tax bracket, in which case it would make better sense to lend to a high-rated municipality.)

Although stockbrokers don't get rich from corporate or municipal bond commissions, either*—and will doubtless try to turn the conversation to stocks when you call, so beware—you should be able to get some advice from your local account representative concerning which bonds to buy. He can, for example, check out the call provisions of different bonds.

Mainly, however, you have to decide for yourself how much risk to take; how many different bonds to buy to spread that risk; and how long you are willing to wait to redeem the bonds at par value.

For tax purposes you may wish to buy bonds that were issued years ago at low "coupon rates"—for example, $45 interest per $1,000 bond—and which, accordingly, will be selling at deep discounts from their $1,000 par value. When those bonds mature (which

---

*Brokers typically charge around $5 to buy or sell a bond, with a $25 minimum, and if you hold them to maturity, there is no commission to pay when they are redeemed. Brokerage commissions for buying or selling an equivalent amount of stock can be four or five times as much.

you could time to coincide roughly with your children's college years or your retirement), you will receive the full $1,000 face value. And that profit—the difference between the $650 you paid for the bond, say, and the $1,000 it paid off at maturity—is taxed as a long-term capital gain.

There are bond mutual funds—both **corporate bond funds** and tax-free **municipal bond funds**—that do the choosing for you and provide much greater diversification than you ever could. However, some charge sales commissions or redemption fees, and all charge management fees. Unless that management fee is awfully low (½% or less), as a few are, it's hard to justify paying it.

It's one thing to pay a management fee to one of the short-term money-market funds described earlier: for that fee you get a fair amount of service as you move your money in and out, and you get an opportunity to participate in instruments denominated in enormous amounts you could never afford yourself. But with corporate or municipal bonds you plan to buy once and hold a long time, the management fees are harder to justify. It's just as easy to call a broker and buy five bonds each in five different issues—$25,000 worth in all, on which the total commission should be about $125—as it is to purchase shares in a bond fund and then pay as much as 1%—$250—*year after year* as a management fee. As for expertise in choosing the bonds, you may be able to tell the difference between AAA and Baa almost as well as an expert.

Dreyfus has a tax-exempt bond fund that charges up to .95% in annual management fees. Considering that high-quality municipals may yield as little as 5% on average, taking nearly 1% off the top means skimming off nearly a fifth of the tax-free income you would have gotten if you had bypassed the fund and bought your high-quality bonds directly through a broker. (Your broker's firm should have a municipal bond expert on staff, too, if it makes you feel any better.)

Unit trusts are bond mutual funds that are *not* managed. Whatever corporate or municipal bonds the trust starts out with are the bonds which, barring any defaults, are eventually redeemed at the other end. As a result, there is no management fee to speak of. There is generally a sales commission, however, of from 2.5 to 4.5%.

Unit trusts are put together with different maturities. They can be found advertised in such papers as *Barron's* and the *Wall Street Journal*. They do provide diversification. However, some of the trusts will accept risks, such as hospital bonds backed solely by the revenue of the hospital (and not by the taxing power of the city or county it is located in), that you yourself might not. The man who assembles the package of bonds is more concerned that the yield look attractive, so it sells, than that twelve years from now, when he is long gone, the bonds remain safe.

Once sold to the public, unit trusts are not traded. Investors may redeem their shares with the trustee at "net asset value"—at a loss if bond prices have fallen since the trust was issued, at a profit if they have risen.

Convertible debentures are bonds that pay you a specified interest rate, but also give you the right to convert your bonds into a given number of shares of common stock. That's what's known as an "equity kicker." With a convertible bond, you have a chance to both sleep *and* eat well. In tough times, unless the company goes bankrupt altogether, you still get your specified interest on the bond; but should the company strike it rich, you could profit along with the common shareholders.

Preferred stocks are like bonds—they pay a fixed dividend—but they never "mature." They are like a permanent loan and not, as their name implies, a piece of the action. They are "preferred" only in that their dividend must be paid in full before any dividend on common stock may be paid; and if the company fails, preferred shareholders come ahead of common shareholders—but behind an awful lot of others, such as bondholders—if anything remains to be split up. What preferreds do not provide is an opportunity to participate in the company's good fortune, should it have any (unless it is a "convertible preferred"). The dividend never goes up.

A "cumulative preferred" is one that promises to pay its dividend no matter what, even if it can't be paid on time. The dividend may be omitted if necessary, but it is still owed to the preferred stockholders, and no common-stock dividends may be paid until all the preferred dividends are paid off. In the case of a company that flirted with bankruptcy for a few years, the arrearage could be substantial—and an investor who gambled on the preferred at giveaway prices could profit handsomely if the company ever righted itself. LTV Corp., the steel-meatpacking-aerospace conglomerate, which is still not the world's most financially sound, has a $5 cumulative preferred which once sold for as much as $202 a share (1967), but which you could have bought a few years later (1971) for $17. The dividends had stopped—but they were "cumulating," should the company ever recover. In 1975, $22.50 a share in back dividends was paid out to the then preferred shareholders, and the $5 dividend was resumed.

Of course, this kind of speculation is hardly what you would have called minimal risk.

By and large, preferred stocks are not good investments for individuals. One reason is that *corporate* investors bid them up in price. To corporations, but not individuals, preferreds provide an important tax advantage, and hence are worth a premium. Why should *you* pay a premium for a tax break that doesn't apply to you?

Tax-deferred annuities are offered by insurance companies as a means of setting up retirement funds for people who can't set up the kinds of plans described in the next chapter.

Under such plans, as of this writing, you are paid around 7 or 8% on your savings—*but the rate could fall once you've been hooked in the program.* It is often not guaranteed beyond the first year. Your money compounds without your having to pay tax on it until you withdraw it, presumably at retirement, when you will be in a lower tax bracket. However, in addition to their paying only a modest interest rate, the insurance companies charge either a sales fee at the outset or a redemption fee when you want out.

If you bought municipals instead, your money would not earn as high a rate (at least not initially), but neither would you *ever* have to pay taxes on it, nor any sales or redemption fee.

If you are in a high enough tax bracket, have your life insurance agent explain the additional features of the "single-premium deferred annuity contract," as it is called—but think twice before buying.

IMPORTANT NOTE:
Getting a high rate of interest doesn't help if you don't save money in the first place. Many people won't save unless "forced" to. For this reason, a payroll-savings plan or whole life insurance contract, or some other form of poor-return saving (for years savings

bank Christmas Clubs paid no interest at all!) may be better than planning to buy bonds or stocks and never getting around to doing it.

What's more, not all payroll savings plans are to be sniffed at. Sixty of the 100 largest industrial companies in the U.S. offer some form of payroll savings plan, with the savings typically being invested either in savings bonds or the company's own stock. Not only do such plans enjoy tax advantages, *in more than half the cases the companies themselves kick in 50 cents or $1 for each $1 the employee contributes!* If your employer is so generous, by all means take full advantage of it. You can be sure no savings bank or stockbroker is going to give you 50 cents outright for each dollar you save!

CHAPTER 4

The People's Loophole

*If I had put just two million into that deal, I'd
be a rich man today.*

                    —A real estate man we know

If you have young children, here is one good way to
have your savings compound tax-free:

Save money in *their* names, with their Social Security numbers on the savings or brokerage accounts,
and let *them* pay taxes on the interest or dividends
that accrue. As most six-year-olds are in the zero-
percent tax bracket, there will be no tax due on the
interest or dividends. Their savings for college will
mount tax-free.*

You can give each child up to $3,000 a year without
having to pay gift tax. Of course, the money then be-
longs to them, not you, both interest and principal.
But if you were going to spend it on them anyway,
what difference does it make?

As custodian of the child's savings or brokerage account, you have the right to withdraw funds at any
time to spend on the child's behalf. Or you can leave
the money in savings certificates, stocks, or bonds to
grow. The child may *not* touch the money—only the
custodian may. You are not required to relinquish
custodianship of the accounts until the child turns 18

---

*You may obtain a Social Security number for your child from your
local Social Security Administration office. All you need is the child's
birth certificate. Filing a tax return for the child each year is also a very
simple matter.

or 21, depending on your state's age of maturity (although you may do so sooner if you wish), by which time you may have chosen to spend the entire fund on his or her tuition, room, and board (summer camp, clothing, braces—whatever).

If you were in the 40% tax bracket and saved $1,000 a year for 18 years at 8% interest in your children's names, your $18,000 would have accumulated $22,441 in compounded after-tax interest—versus just $10,936 if you saved the money in your own name.

Either way, you set aside $1,000 a year; this way you come out $11,505 ahead. Just by doing your bookkeeping a little differently.*

It's not a bad loophole, but this chapter is about an even better set, having to do with your retirement. *Even if you are still just a college student, earning several hundred dollars a year, I urge you to read this section.* If you wait until you're nearing retirement, it will be too late.

First the bad news:

As you probably know, all the money you've been paying in Social Security taxes, lo these many years, has not been set aside for your retirement. It has been paid out to people who are already in retirement. It's gone. The way the system works, when your golden years roll around, some other generation of workers will be paying taxes to support you. Which is fine except for two things. First, even at current levels Social Security benefits are more peanut butter than caviar. Second, by the time today's 30- and 40-year-olds are ready to retire, the population of this country will have shifted dramatically: Instead of having lots of workers working to support relatively few retirees— as things stand now—you are going to have relatively

---

*If you already have substantial assets, you might prefer to set up what is known as a Clifford Trust. The income from the trust goes to the child and is taxed at his rate, but the principal eventually reverts back to you. Ask your accountant or attorney about this.

few under-65s working to support hoards of retirees. It's hard to imagine how even the current level of support will be maintained.

What this means is that if we want to live nicely, we will all have to provide, in large measure, for ourselves. The good news is that Congress has made it a lot easier for us to do so. Although ERISA, the pension reform act of 1974, is the most complicated law ever written—bureaucracy and the legal system run wild —it boils down to this: If you already have a pension plan where you work, you are less likely to get screwed out of your share of its benefits than you once were; and if you don't already have a pension plan at work —or if you have earnings apart from your salary— you can start one of your own.

There are two kinds. If you have income from self-employment, you may set up a Keogh Plan. If you do not have such income, but are not covered by a pension plan at work either, you may set up an Individual Retirement Account (IRA).

There are very few truly good things in the world, but if you qualify, these are two of them. In fact, anyone who qualifies to set up a Keogh Plan or IRA and doesn't is making a very big mistake.

With either plan, the income you contribute each year is exempted from taxes. So, too, the interest, dividends, and capital gains those contributions accrue. It is only when you begin withdrawing money from the plan, any time after you are 59½, that you pay taxes on what you take out. But by then, the assumption is, you are likely to be retired or semiretired and so in a relatively low tax bracket. Even if you're not, your savings will have been allowed to compound much faster than they otherwise could have.

Let's say you are 29½ and you contribute $1,000 to a Keogh Plan or IRA next week. At 8% tax-free it would compound to $10,062 by the time you were

59½. Then, when you withdrew it—particularly if you had just retired and weren't earning much other taxable income (Social Security benefits are not counted as taxable income)—perhaps 30% of what you withdrew would go to taxes, leaving you with $7,043.

If you had *not* contributed that $1,000 to a Keogh Plan or IRA when you earned it, aged 29½, the first thing that would have happened is that it would have been taxed. If you were in the 40% bracket, $400 would immediately have gone to the government, leaving you $600. If you had then invested that $600 at 8% a year, it would have grown—after taxes—at just under 5%. Thirty years later, aged 59½—assuming you had resisted the temptation to blow the money on a terrific Caribbean cruise or a bogus cosmetics franchise—it would have grown to $2,449.

The first way you are left with $7,043; the second way, starting with the exact same $1,000 in income and assuming the exact same 8% rate of interest, a mere $2,449. The Keogh Plan or IRA leaves you with more than two-and-a-half times as much money after tax, even though it requires absolutely no more to start with, no more risk or effort, and, in fact, *less* self-discipline. (Because once it's locked up in the plan, you will not constantly be tempted to do something different with it.)

If you put that $1,000 into such a plan at age 25 instead of 29½, and waited to begin withdrawing it until you were 65 instead of 59½, under the same assumptions the Keogh Plan or IRA would leave you with more than $15,000 after-tax, versus a mere $3,914.

And that's just $1,000, one year. If you contribute that much—or more—year after year, you are talking hundreds of thousands of dollars, as the table on the next page shows.

The prime thing to note from this table is the importance of starting early. Indeed, the contributions in your later years will add relatively little to the value of your fund. It is the early contributions which, compounded over time, grow enormously. You could, for example, contribute $1,000 a year from age 20 to 35 and then nothing. If you then withdrew the money between the ages of 65 and 75, your initial $15,000 would have grown (at 8% interest) to provide you a total of more than $400,000!

So why doesn't everyone who qualifies for such a plan set one up, either at his local savings bank, stock brokerage firm, or life insurance company, and contribute to it to the maximum extent allowed? The primary objection comes from people who don't want to

If you contribute $1,000 a year * to a Keogh or IRA for the next . . .	. . and if you can invest it at 8%, this is what you'll have, before taxes, when you begin withdrawing it:	Here's what the same savings would be worth, after taxes, without Keogh or IRA (assuming you are in the 40% bracket):
1 year	$1,080	$629
5 years	$6,335	$3,461
10 years	$15,645	$7,835
15 years	$29,323	$13,366
20 years	$49,421	$20,356
25 years	$78,951	$29,195
30 years	$122,341	$40,369
35 years	$186,097	$54,494
40 years	$279,774	$72,351
45 years	$417,417	$94,925

NOTE: A crucial assumption here is a steadily available 8% rate of interest. If interest rates average even higher, the payouts will be higher; if lower, lower. *But no matter what interest rates are, tax-free interest will grow much faster than taxed interest!*

*To figure what would happen if you contributed $2,000 a year, just double all the numbers; $3,000, triple—and so forth.

tie up their money so long. You may not withdraw money from either the Keogh Plan or IRA until you turn 59½ without incurring a "stiff penalty." For most of us, who can't even plan our finances two months in advance, let alone two decades, this seems hopelessly far off in the future.

Yet there are two very strong arguments against that objection. In the first place, you *can* withdraw money from these plans. The penalty is 10% of what you withdraw, all of which is then taxed as income (the 10% excise tax is *not* deductible). And—in the case of the Keogh Plan—you are disqualified from making contributions to the plan for five years. But you would have had to pay taxes on that income, anyway, if you hadn't put it into the plan—so that part isn't so terrible. And 10%, while indeed a stiff penalty, may not be much to pay for having been allowed to compound your savings—as well as the portion the government would have taken—tax-deferred for several years.

Second and most important: Do you plan to have *any* money saved up by the time you are 59½? *Any* net worth? *Anything* to supplement your Social Security and the generosity of your children? If so—and for most people the answer is an emphatic yes—it may as well be in the form of a tax-free retirement fund. *What can you lose by not paying taxes?*

Unquestionably, a great deal we cannot anticipate will occur over the time spans we are speaking of here. Tax laws are bound to change; U.S. currency could become worthless through spiraling inflation à la Germany in the twenties; we could all be wiped out by epidemic or holocaust. However, none of that is particularly relevant to the question of whether to set up a Keogh Plan or IRA. It is virtually indisputable that whatever investment decisions you make, it's better to make them tax-free than taxable. Further, it is highly unlikely that Congress, no matter what it does with the tax laws, would retroactively penalize the millions of voters who, in good faith, set up tax-deferred retirement funds.

Now down to specifics:

Who qualifies for a Keogh Plan? Anyone with income from self-employment. Doctors, lawyers, dentists, writers, moonlighting policemen, accountants, store owners, barbers, gardeners, free-lancers, consultants, actors, real estate brokers, independent salesmen, decorators, tutors, tennis instructors, photographers: anyone who earns money for himself—not for a boss or employer —by selling a product or service, and whose business is not incorporated. *Even if you have a salaried job, income you earn on the side, on your own, qualifies for a Keogh Plan.*

Who qualifies for an Individual Retirement Account? Anyone who is employed, but who is not already enrolled in a pension plan. (If you are waiting to become eligible for your company's plan, you *may* set up an IRA for the year or two or three that you must wait. However, you cannot contribute to an IRA in any calendar year during which you were covered by a pension plan—even if you were covered for only a small portion of the year.)

How do you find out for sure? Ask at your local savings bank; or call the nearest office of the Internal Revenue Service.

How much can you contribute each year?

IRA: Up to 15% of your earnings each year, but not more than $1,500 ($1,750 if married to a nonworking spouse).

Keogh: Up to 15% of your earnings from self-employment each year, but not more than $7,500. Despite the 15% limitation, *the first $750 of earnings from self-employment is all eligible for the plan.**

Must you contribute that much each year? No. As long as you do not exceed the maximums allowed, you can contribute as much or as little as you want each year—just notify the plan "trustee."

What if you contribute more? You can be fined a penalty of 6% of the excess plus interest—and, of course, that portion of your tax deduction will be disallowed. Note, by the way, that in figuring your "earnings," investment income such as dividends and interest does not count. Also, if you are a dentist who grosses $50,-000 a year but deducts $20,000 of expenses directly related to dentistry, your self-employment income is $30,000 for the purposes of figuring your maximum allowable contribution, not $50,000.

Is there any way to contribute more than $7,500 to a Keogh Plan? Yes. You can set up a "defined benefit." Keogh Plan. IRS regulations in this area are new and somewhat complicated. Consult a good accountant or an experienced life insurance agent.

When do you set up the plan? Today or tomorrow would be the best time, but you have until the last day of the year, for tax purposes.

When do you contribute to the plan? Once the paper work is done to set it up, you may contribute whenever you like during the year—in one lump sum or in many small payments—so long as you don't exceed the maxi-

---

*Unless your adjusted gross income from all sources is greater than $15,000, in which case only a portion of your self-employed earnings (25%) would be eligible to count toward this $750 minimum. If you earn a $35,000 salary but also picked up $2,000 in lecture fees, $500 could be contributed to a Keogh Plan.

mum allowable contribution. In fact, because it is hard
to know just how much that will be until you've done
your taxes, you actually have until April 15 of the
following year to make your contribution to a Keogh
Plan, up to February 14 to contribute to an IRA.
However, the sooner you put money into the plan, the
sooner it begins earning tax-free interest—and over
the years this will mount up into a difference of thousands of dollars. It is a good idea to contribute early
—even January 2—as much as you feel confident of
being allowed to, and then make a final contribution
to bring you up to the limit when you know exactly
how high that limit is.

How much should you contribute? The maximum allowable, if you can possibly afford it. Not to do so is
like throwing money away—unless you enjoy paying
taxes. It may even be prudent, if your basic earning
power is good, to *borrow* some of the cash you need to
take full advantage of the Keogh or IRA deduction.
The interest on your loan is tax-deductible (assuming
you itemize your deductions); whereas the interest that
that money will earn is tax-deferred. Don't borrow at
usurious rates (as at a finance company); but to pay
12% for a few months, tax-deductibly, in order to take
the fullest possible tax deduction for your retirement
fund and earn, say, 8% on it tax-deferred for 30
years—that makes eminent good sense.

Is there any carryover provision? No. Even if you
contribute less than the 15% maximum one year, that
does not entitle you to exceed the 15% limit another
year. It's now or never.

Where can you invest your Keogh or IRA money? Just
about anywhere, as long as some institution acts as
trustee. The best place to go first is any savings bank.

They will provide brochures and answer your questions. Other institutions eager to enroll you in Keogh or IRA retirement plans are mutual funds, life insurance companies, and brokerage firms. Through these you can invest in stocks or bonds. You can even arrange with a brokerage firm to set up a trusteed account which you yourself manage, selecting whichever stocks you wish, and selling them to buy others whenever you like.

You can, moreover, have plans with more than one trustee. You may have some money in a savings bank, other money in a brokerage account, and still other money in a mutual fund. And, within limits, you may transfer money from one trustee to another—just so long as you never take it out of trusteeship for your own uses along the way. Some mutual fund "families" allow you to switch from one to another of their group of funds at will, without changing trustees or incurring special charges.

The most obvious place *not* to invest Keogh or IRA money is in municipal bonds. Why accept their low tax-free yields when anything you put into your retirement fund will grow tax-free anyway? Similarly, because the money grows tax-free and is all taxed as income when it is withdrawn, *dividends and interest are just as valuable as long-term capital gains*—even though ordinarily $1 of long-term capital gains is worth more, after taxes, than $1 of dividends. So there is even more reason than usual to adhere to the bird-in-the-hand philosophy of investing, rather than forgoing current dividends or interest in the hope of realizing large capital gains.

Beyond that, the question of how to invest your retirement money is really the subject of this whole book, not just one or two paragraphs. I began my own Keogh plan at a savings bank, with savings certificates that yield an 8.17% effective rate of interest. It was convenient; the certificates are federally insured; there is no management or "trustee" fee; and mainly, it wasn't much money and I am by nature lazy. When these certificates mature, I may either roll them over at the same bank, with new savings certificates (at the new 8.45% rate), or, more probably, use the money— still sheltered within the Keogh Plan—to buy stocks.

What forms do you fill out? Whichever institution(s) you grace with your business will help you with the red tape. Basically, there is little. On your federal tax return you merely deduct your contributions for the year on the line that says, "Payments to an individual retirement arrangement" and attach the specified form 5329 (which must be filed even in years you made no contributions to your IRA); or the next line, which is for Keogh contributions, and file form 5500K separately. These contributions will lower your "taxable income," and hence your taxes, *whether you itemize deductions or not.*

What does the trustee charge? It varies from nothing, at most savings banks, to quite a lot at some mutual funds. Be sure to find out in advance. Where stocks and bonds are involved, there will be both brokerage commissions, for buying and selling, *and* a fee for the trustee (generally an obscure savings bank with which the brokerage firm has teamed up for the purpose of offering these plans). With life insurance companies, there are likely to be all kinds of extra costs, both explicit and hidden. Watch out! Ordinarily, I would avoid setting up an insurance-company-trusteed plan.

Can you have both a Keogh Plan and an IRA? Yes and no. Even if you have salaried income that qualifies for an IRA and self-employment income on the side, *you cannot contribute to both in any given year.* However, you can establish a Keogh Plan one year and then, if you take a salaried job, cease contributing to it (although it will continue growing), and set up an IRA. Later, if you quit the job, or if your outside earnings from self-employment were large enough, you could resume payments to the Keogh Plan and cease contributing to the IRA.

What is an IRA "rollover" account? This is for people who leave jobs where they have been accruing tax-sheltered pension benefits already. Upon leaving, you are likely to be paid at least some portion of those accrued benefits in a lump sum—which then exposes them to income tax. However, you may be eligible to put the entire sum—regardless of the normal 15%/$1,500 limitations—into an IRA rollover account, to keep from having to pay any tax on the lump sum itself, nor on the interest it will continue to accrue. Check your local bank for details.

What if, self-employed now, you later become employed? You can no longer make contributions to your Keogh Plan (unless you still are earning some money on the side, apart from your job); but what you have already contributed to the fund keeps growing, tax-free.

What if your employer enrolls you in a pension plan? You can no longer contribute to your IRA; but the money you've already contributed keeps growing, tax-free.

What if you are both employed? If a husband and wife are both employed by companies that do not cover them with a pension plan, then each may have his or her own IRA up to a maximum of $1,500 a year—for a total combined tax shelter of up to $3,000 a year. This is true even though they file a joint tax return.

What if you are both self-employed? If both spouses have self-employment income, *each* is entitled to contribute up to $7,500 a year—even if they file jointly.

Can you borrow against the value of your fund? Not in the sense of putting it up as collateral. This is strictly forbidden. However, if when you go for a personal loan it is evident that you have thousands, or even tens or hundreds of thousands of dollars saved up in a retirement plan—which you could draw on, with penalties, if you had to—it will obviously help you get the loan. Especially because:

Can your fund be taken from you by creditors if you go bankrupt? Yes.

When can you begin withdrawing your money? To avoid penalty you must wait until you are at least 59½. However, you are not *required* to begin withdrawing it until you are 70½, at which point you must.

Must you be retired? No. At least not as far as the IRS is concerned. However, some Keogh Plan trustees do make this a provision of their plan, so find out in advance.

How is the money withdrawn? Your funds may be withdrawn all at once, or over a period of years that is keyed to your life expectancy (or the combined life expectancy of you and your spouse). Choosing the latter method allows the balance to continue to compound tax-free. With a Keogh Plan (but not an IRA), if you do withdraw the money all at once, it is taxed, mercifully, under special income-averaging regulations that greatly reduce the bite. (To qualify for these special regulations, you must have been a participant in a Keogh Plan for at least the previous five years.)

What if you die or become disabled? Upon death or disability—regardless of your age—the entire fund may be withdrawn, either all at once or over a period of years.

What if you have employees? If you set up a Keogh Plan for yourself you are required by law to make contributions for your employees' retirements as well as your own. However, you can set up the plan in such a way that your employees do not become eligible to participate until they have been working for you for three years. Check the local savings bank for details.

What if you have partners? If your income is derived from partnerships, there are further regulations—ask your accountant. The partnership—not you individually—must set up the Keogh Plan, even though one or more partners may elect not to participate. What's more, if you are involved with more than one partnership, you may be required to set up retirement plans for the others if you set one up for one. Check the details.

What if you are already over 59½? It's not too late to set up one of these retirement plans—and the tax savings can still be substantial.

Further questions? Write the nearest Internal Revenue Service office for IRS publication 590 and struggle through it, or ask the retirement expert at your savings bank to help you. Also, for complicated situations—if you are an employer thinking of setting up a plan for your company, or if you are involved in one or more partnerships—I recommend Steven Anreder's *How-To Retire Rich Before 60* ($8.95, Farnsworth Publishing

Company, 78 Randall Avenue, Rockville Center, NY 11570), which is devoted entirely to this subject. It is excellent.

Retirement plans are not a way to grow rich slowly, let alone quick. If interest rates *do* stay high (or go even higher), it will only be because inflation simultaneously eats steadily away at purchasing power. Thus $500,000 in 30 or 40 years may well be like $100,000 now—a lot, but not "rich." If interest rates decline, you will be locked into high rates on what you contribute now (if you choose long-term bonds or stocks whose dividends are maintained or increased) —but you won't be able to reinvest the income those contributions generate at the same high rates, and so you won't have $500,000 after all.

Neither way will you be "rich." But either way you could well be comfortable, and that's very nearly as good.

Part Two

The Stock Market

CHAPTER 5

Meanwhile Down at the Track

October. This is one of the peculiarly dangerous
months to speculate in stocks. Others are November, December, January, February, March, April,
May, June, July, August, and September.

—Mark Twain

OK. You have some money in a savings bank; you
have set up a Keogh Plan or Individual Retirement
Account, if possible, and are contributing to it at the
maximum rate allowed; you have equity in a home, if
you want it; you've tied up $1,000 in bulk purchases
of tunafish and shaving cream; you have lowered your
auto and homeowner's insurance premiums by increasing your "deductibles"; you have adequate term life
insurance; you've paid off all your 18% installment
loans (and most of your 12% loans); there is a little
Hitachi water heater sitting on your roof above your
well-insulated attic; and you own enough AT&T (or
some other solid common, or even preferred, stock) to
take full advantage of the $100 ($200) dividend
tax exclusion. In short, you have done all the things that
scream to be done. You have made the easy decisions.

Now what?

There are three compelling reasons to invest in stocks.

1. *Over the long run—and it may be very long—
stocks should outperform bonds.* The reason is that
stock and bond prices are set in the open market—
and the market, over the long run, rewards risk. From

1926 to 1975, the total compounded annual rate of return you would have had from buying risk-free United States Treasury bills was 2.3%; the return from slightly riskier corporate bonds would have been 3.8%, and the return from stocks would have been 9%. The compounded annual rate of inflation during the same period was 2.3%. Ignoring taxes, $1,000 invested in corporate bonds over that time span would have grown to $6,200, and to $68,200 if invested in stocks.

Of course, you can play with numbers like these, depending on the time periods you choose. There were some pretty dreadful five- and ten-year stretches nestled in among those 50 years, during which you would have been much better off in bonds or even a savings account. Timing is very important. Granted, too, the ability of equity (stocks) to outperform debt (bonds) —and to beat inflation—during those fifty years had much to do with America's steadily improving productivity, which is unlikely to improve as rapidly in the next fifty years. The world has changed. Resources are scarcer; unions are stronger; businesses are more highly regulated; confidence in the future, and hence investment, is not what it once was; inflation is pernicious; and, because of inflation, bond rates are a great deal higher than that 3.8% fifty-year average. At this writing it's not hard to find high-grade bonds that guarantee to do nearly as well over the next twenty or thirty years—8 or 9% interest—as stocks did over the past fifty. Yet the fact remains that over the long run, because the market *knows* all these things, stocks will be priced low enough to offer buyers reason to buy.

2. *Unlike bonds, stocks offer at least the potential of keeping up with inflation,* even if that potential is by no means always realized. Once the interest rate on a bond is set, it's set. Bread could go to $2 a loaf, and the bond wouldn't pay a nickel more in interest. But

ITT, which owns the company that bakes the bread, might—might—be able to keep its profits, and its dividend, rising in step with inflation.

3. *If all goes well, stocks can act as a tax shelter.* Long-term capital gains are taxed at about only half the rate of ordinary income. But more than that, by choosing a stock that pays out little or none of its profits in dividends, you pay little or no tax on your share of those profits. Instead, the company retains those profits and reinvests them for you. If they do so profitably—in a great new product or a more efficient factory, say—future profits, and your share of them, will be even larger. This is the bird-in-the-bush strategy of investing. One of its drawbacks derives from the fact that corporate accounting, even when practiced with pure motives, is a matter of judgment, at best. The only profit statement you can truly bank on is a dividend check that doesn't bounce.

Nonetheless, with this bird-in-the-bush strategy you can ultimately profit two ways. First, after a period of years the company you've invested in may decide to pay out a greater portion of its (by-then-greater) profits as dividends. You will then have to pay income tax on those dividends, but in the meantime you've been reinvesting, through the company, money the government would otherwise have taken. Second, you can sell your stock. If the company has indeed invested your profits wisely, there is a chance, but by no means a certainty, that you will get more for it than you paid—perhaps even several times as much. And that profit, if a long-term capital gain, will be taxed at just half the normal rate.

It thus becomes a matter of some interest just how well a company is likely to reinvest all those profits they don't pay you as dividends. Unfortunately, there is no way to know for sure. However, you can determine how well they've done—or, because accounting is open to so much qualification and interpretation, *seem* to have done—in the past. The number you are looking for is "return on equity," and it is, simply, the company's profits expressed as a percentage of all the money shareholders have dumped in over the years, much of it by forgoing dividends.

There are companies like IBM which have been able to reinvest those accumulated unpaid dividends at returns well above 15% a year; and there are others, like B. F. Goodrich, that have earned less than 5% on the money left with them. And then there are the Penn Centrals, which have diddled it away altogether.

Naturally, investors would much prefer stock in companies like the former than the latter, all other things being equal. So all other things are *not* equal: You have to pay more for stock in companies that are known to reinvest profits at a high rate of return. Indeed, there was a time when you had to pay $60 or more to get a $1 slice of Avon's profit pie, so excited were investors by Avon's ability to earn 25 to 30% on that $1.* At the same time it cost only $8 to buy a $1 slice of Goodrich's profit pie. What investors failed to note was that, while 25% was a boffo return on that one reinvested Avon dollar, $1—no matter how well it was reinvested—was a pretty lousy return on a $60 investment! Subsequently Avon stock fell about 75% even though profits kept growing admirably, and as I write this you have to pay "only" $17 for a $1 slice of Avon's ever-growing profit pie.†

So there's more to choosing the right stock than finding the company with the highest "return on equity." But I'm getting ahead of myself. I should not talk like this until you know as much about the essentials of the stock market—the forest—as the professionals

*Avon was earning a little over $2 in profit for each of its shares. The shares went for $140 apiece.

†$47 a share, each of which earned nearly $3.

do. This will take up most of the rest of the chapter. (Getting to know as much about the trees could take up most of the rest of your life.)

The stock market could hardly be simpler. There are just two ways a stock can go: up or down. There are just two emotions that tug in those opposite directions: greed and fear. There are just two ways to make money on a stock: dividends and capital gains. And there are just two kinds of investors in the market: the "public," like you or me; and the "institutions," like bank trust departments and mutual funds and insurance companies. It's the amateurs against the professionals, and it's not at all clear who has the advantage. Often, both lose. Finally—and here it gets only slightly more complicated—there are just three kinds of stocks:

1. There are 300 or 400 stocks that the institutions keep tabs on and eagerly invest in. These command premium prices, although not the way they once did, in the early seventies, when Avon was selling for 60 times its profits. You should avoid these stocks, as they can hardly represent "overlooked value."

2. There are perhaps another 300 or 400 stocks the institutions follow but do not invest in with any enthusiasm. They are out of fashion, and thus at least worth considering. Some day they could return to fashion.

3. And then there are the overwhelming majority of stocks that the institutions neither follow nor invest in but simply ignore. These are called the bottom-tier stocks, because they have been relegated to the pits. Some of them, under certain circumstances, may be worth your investing in.

All stocks fall into another three categories, as well. They are all either overvalued, fairly valued, or undervalued.

To suggest any correlation between these two sets of categories—to suggest, that is, that institutional favorites are overvalued, middle-tier stocks fairly valued, and bottom-tier stocks undervalued—would, of course, be the height of oversimplification, not to mention financial heresy. Still, it's a thought to keep in mind.

What is a stock worth? Market veterans will tell you that a stock is worth whatever people are willing to pay for it. Price is determined by supply and demand. If lots of people want it, it will be worth a lot. If everyone ignores it, it won't be worth spitting at.

But it is too simple to say that a stock is worth whatever people will pay for it, because what people are willing to pay for it depends, in turn, on what they think it is worth. It is a circular definition, and one that is used as a rationalization of financial foolishness rather than as a rational way to appraise value.

The value of a stock should not be nearly so subjective as, say, the value of a Picasso sketch or a 1909S VDB penny. Rather than entitling its owner to some inestimable esthetic pleasure or some irreplaceable rarity, a share of stock merely entitles the owner to a share of present and future profits (or, in the event of bankruptcy or acquisition by another company, assets). Where two paintings of equal size may reasonably command vastly different values, two companies of equal profits, assets, and prospects should not. Yet they do.

The market veteran will readily agree that this is irrational, but he will ask you, with a laugh, "Who ever said the stock market was rational?"

That gets the market veteran off the hook and may eliminate in his mind the need to search for value. But there are other market veterans, perhaps even a majority by now, who believe that over the long run rationality does pay off in the market. Sooner or later, they say, bubbles burst; sooner or later bargains are recognized as such. A company cannot prosper forever without its shareholders at some point benefiting.

Indeed, if the market is driven by irrational greed and fear to excesses of over- and undervaluation, as it surely is, then it is the rational man, they say, seeing these excesses for what they are, who will be buying the excessively undervalued stock, particularly when the market as a whole is depressed; and selling the excessively overvalued stock, particularly when the market as a whole is on high ground. Thus may he profit from the swings in between.

All of this assumes that a rational man can determine what a stock is "really" worth.

Rational men differ. A company's future prospects —and even its current profits—are open to widely differing assessments. Obviously, no one can answer precisely what a stock is worth. But that doesn't eliminate the need to arrive at some rational valuation, nor the possibility of setting some reasonable guidelines for doing so.

What a stock is worth depends at any given time on the alternative investments that are then available. It is a question of relative value. Think of investments as wallets. A 5% savings account is a wallet you can buy for $20 that miraculously fills up with $1 (5%) by the end of every year. It is convenient—you can "sell" it whenever you want and be sure of getting back your full $20—but it's not a great investment. At the time of this writing you can buy other "wallets" that fill up with the same $1 just as fast—not for $20 but for a mere $12.50. Namely, long-term savings certificates or high-grade corporate bonds that pay 8% interest.

You can say the first wallet sells for "20 times earnings" and the second for "12.5 times earnings." This is the famous "price/earnings ratio," or "multiple," you have heard so much about, although it's generally applied to stocks, not bonds or wallets.*

Now. If a virtually risk-free investment like an AT&T bond sells for 12 or 13 times earnings, what should a stock sell for?

On the one hand, a stock should sell for *less,* because it involves more risk. There is no guarantee that the $1 will show up in the wallet by the end of the year—or even that the wallet itself will be in any shape for you to sell it to someone else, should you so desire. What's more, only a portion of your $1 is actually paid out to you as a cash dividend. Much, most, or all of it may be retained by the company.

On the other hand, a stock should perhaps sell for *more,* because it involves more potential reward (either the earnings or stock price could go *up*) and because of the tax advantages referred to earlier.

In deciding how much more or less to pay for a stock than the 12 or 13 times earnings you pay for a savings certificate or high-grade bond—or whatever the going rate is at the time you read this—one weighs the extra risk against the potential for extra return.

For stock in a moribund company whose earnings seem likely to decline each year right into bankruptcy, you would not pay very much no matter how good past earnings may have been.

For stock in a company whose earnings over the long run seem about as likely to increase as to decrease—where risk and reward about cancel one another out—you might expect to pay 12 or 13 times earnings. So if you find such a stock selling for 5 or 6 times earnings—as many do—it could look pretty good.

For stock in a company whose earnings seem likely to be able to keep pace with inflation—no "real"

---

*You will find every stock's "p/e ratio" listed, along with its dividend and price, in the stock pages of most newspapers.

growth, that is, but growth in earnings all the same—
you might expect to pay more than the 12 or 13 times
earnings you would pay for a high-grade bond, the
earnings of which do not rise with inflation. In fact,
companies like this have also sold recently at 5 or 6
times earnings. A bargain? You bet.

Finally, for stock in a company whose prospects
are really bright, with the possibility of real growth of
5% or 10% or even 20% a year for the foreseeable
future, you might expect to pay a lot more than 12 or
13 times earnings—as the banks did with Avon. One
serious problem, however, is that the future has consistently proved remarkably unforeseeable. There are always loads of well-reasoned and seemingly conservative
projections around; but the funniest things happen on
the way to the future.

All other things being equal—that is, if *all* stocks
were selling at 12 or 13 times earnings—you would
choose only those companies whose earnings were expected to grow the fastest. But the question is not
whether a fast-growing company is better than a slow-
growing one. Any idiot knows that IBM is a "better"
company than U.S. Shoe. The question is whether you should pay 15 to 20 times earnings for the one
or 4 to 6 times earnings for the other. Which stock, at
any given time, is a better *relative value?* The real
trick—and payoff—is to find a company selling for 6
times earnings that you think will grow as fast as the
one selling for 20 times earnings. Then you know for
sure which one to buy.

Admittedly, it's not quite this simple. For one thing,
it makes sense to look not just at what a company
may earn, but also at what it *owns.* A company whose
business is lousy, but which happens to be conducted
on 50,000 acres of wholly owned real estate between
Dallas and Fort Worth, might have a liquidation value
—if you closed down the business and paid off all the

creditors—of $25 a share. Yet such land might be valued on the company's books at next to nothing, if it had been acquired earlier in the century—so it might not even show up in quick calculations of the company's "book value." It could be what's known as a hidden asset, and well worth buying a share in, regardless of the company's dismal earnings.

I should also point out that the 12 or 13 times earnings I've been using as a benchmark is by no means eternal. It all depends on what wallets are going for at any given time. If you can get 9.5% from a high-grade 20-year corporate bond—or by paying off the balance of your 9.5% 20-year mortgage, for that matter, which amounts to much the same thing—then you have a low-risk wallet that produces $1 for every $10.50 you put up—10½ times earnings. The higher the prevailing interest rate on savings certificates or high-grade corporate bonds—or mortgage prepayments —the less you should be willing to pay for stocks. And vice versa.

Now it happens that far from looking at assets or relative value, the professional money managers of the late sixties and early seventies—particularly those at the banks, which manage tens of billions of dollars of other people's money—concentrated their attention and their megabucks on a relative handful of fast-growing companies, bidding their prices up to truly remarkable heights. The "nifty fifty," these stocks were called—"glamour" stocks, "one-decision" stocks (you just had to decide to buy them; you would never sell them, no matter what price you could get). The group included such indisputably fine companies as Polaroid, Disney, Avon, IBM, Coca-Cola, Kodak, Xerox, and McDonald's.

Most stocks they ignored altogether. Not because they lacked merit—although, admittedly, some of them did—but because it's a lot less trouble to put

$100 million into Johnson & Johnson than to stay late at the office each night hunting for 50 less visible companies—perhaps better values—in which to invest $2 million each. The first rule of fiduciary bureaucracy was (and largely still is): You can't be criticized for losing money in IBM. Corollary: He who does what everyone else does will not do appreciably worse. In other words, it was *unfortunate* to lose money in IBM, Avon, Tropicana, or Levitz Furniture; but it would have been *imprudent* to lose somewhat less money in the stocks of companies no one ever heard of.

In talking with people who managed billions of dollars at some of the nation's largest banks during this period, I got the distinct impression that it would have been *undignified* for top-drawer financial institutions like theirs to invest in anything but large, top-drawer American corporations.

That posture has a fiduciary ring to it, until you consider how much extra the banks were paying to invest in such firms, and how much they ultimately lost for their clients by doing so.

One money manager from a major New York bank told me that it was his bank's policy to invest only in companies whose earnings they expected to grow at an above-average rate. What about companies they expected to grow at only an average or subaverage rate? No, he said, they did not buy stock in such companies. Regardless of price? Regardless of price. Was there *any* price at which the bank would buy stock in an average-growth company?

This question made the money manager uncomfortable. He clearly wanted to answer no, because he clearly would be damned before he would buy stock in such a company. But he couldn't come right out and say that, because he knew that, theoretically, there must be *some* price at which he should choose the stock of the mediocre company over the stocks of his nifty fifty.

It's not that the bank had compared some of the low-multiple stocks with some of the high-multiple stocks and decided consciously that, yes, the high-multiple stocks represented a better value despite their premium prices. Rather, the policy (dogma?) was based on studies that showed how, over the long run, the best way to beat the stock market averages had been to buy stock in companies whose earnings grew faster than average. That's how things had worked in the past, and that's why 51% of this bank's discretionary billions were invested in just 14 stocks, only one of which, at the time of our luncheon, was selling for less than 20 times earnings.

At one point in this madness, in fact, a few years ago, you had a great many of the nation's otherwise intelligent, well-educated, exceptionally well-bred and well-paid fiduciaries valuing the Avon Corporation more highly than the Ford Motor Company and Gulf + Western Industries *combined*. This despite the fact that Ford and Gulf + Western had $25 billion in sales to Avon's $1 billion; $15 billion in assets to Avon's $700 million; and $1 billion in profits to Avon's $135 million. Not only that, Ford and Gulf + Western were paying out $280 million a year in dividends that year, compared with $85 million for Avon.

It was true that if Avon continued to grow at its then-average 14% a year, and if Ford and Gulf + Western grew more slowly, Avon's profits would have grown to equal the combined profits of the other two in a mere 25 years or so (although in the meantime it would have paid out much less in dividends). But why wait 25 years for profits which, for the same money, the money managers could have owned then and there?

Since then, Avon and stocks like it have fallen sharply in price, while Ford and Gulf + Western and others like them have done much better. But what's important is not that you should have shorted Avon back then and bought Ford (although you would indeed have made a killing); what's important is that this sort of irrational imbalance could have occurred at all.

On Wall Street it happens all the time, if not always on such a grand scale. And herein, I suggest, may lie an opportunity.

Even though the major institutions, which account for two-thirds or more of the trading in stocks, have of late been searching much more widely for good values than they were in the early seventies, there are still a great many companies that are largely or entirely ignored—*whether they are exceptional values or not.*

Subject to the caveats and additional suggestions in the next chapters, here is what for most people has to be about the most sensible way to invest in stocks, if they are going to invest in stocks at all:

1. To begin with, only invest money you won't have to touch, if need be, for many years. Retirement is not a great time to start buying stocks. People who buy stocks when they get bonuses and sell them when the roof starts to leak are entrusting their investment decisions to their roofs.

(One kind of money you won't be touching for years is the money stashed away in your Keogh Plan, should you be lucky enough to have one.)

2. Buy low and sell high. You laugh. Yet even though this is quite obviously the key to success, most people, particularly small investors, shun the market when it is getting drubbed and venture back only after it has recovered and appears, once again, to be "healthy."

It is precisely when the market looks worst that the opportunities are best; precisely when things are good again that the opportunities are slimmest and the risks greatest.

Item: At what was probably the most opportune time to buy stocks since the Great Depression, December of 1974, with the Dow Jones industrial average struggling to break above 600 and countless lesser stocks selling for a half or a third or even a quarter of their book values, financial columnist Eliot Janeway was advising small investors to stay away. "No investment market in the coming year," he said with his customary self-assurance, "is going to be safe for civilians." In point of fact, the Dow climbed 40% in 1975, and many of the stocks that had been battered far worse than the Dow "blue chips" doubled and tripled.

Item: A Washington, D.C., investment club purchased 200 shares of a stock at 18. "Club sold all holdings at 12½," it reported to *Black Enterprise* magazine, "*due to decline in price;* intends to reinvest *when price moves up.*" (Italics mine.) What kind of strategy is *that?*

Torn as we all are between greed and fear, we tend to do just the wrong thing. When the economy is sinking fast and stocks faster, we get more and more scared. Finally, we quit in disgust. Better to get out with a big loss, we say to ourselves, than to watch our holdings collapse altogether. In fact, of course, this is just the time to be getting into the market, not out of it.

By the same token, avoid investing when the market is generally judged to be healthy, when you are becoming excited by the gains in some of the stocks you already own, when prospects for the economy are generally conceded to be bright, and when people are talking about the real possibility that the Dow Jones industrial average will finally break through to new ground. *In such a climate people are expecting good news. If it comes, it won't move the market much because it has been so widely anticipated.* If, by chance, bad news should come instead, that will move the market—down.

Whether concerning an individual stock, or the market as a whole, always ask yourself which would be more of a surprise: good news or bad news. News that is expected never has as much impact—if any at all—as news that is not.

"The truth is," writes market analyst Dr. Martin Zweig,

that the stock market does best when earnings and dividends are getting drubbed, and worst when [they] are zooming. For example, look at very recent history: In the fourth quarter of 1972 and the first quarter of 1973 . . . earnings of the Dow Industrials soared upward by 35% over year-earlier periods. The market responded by crashing more violently than at any time since the 'thirties. Then, amid the depths of pessimism, first- and second-quarter 1975 Dow profits collapsed an average of 31%; yet the stock market simultaneously vaulted 43%, one of the best six-month surges in history.

"One reason that so many investors get overloaded with stocks at market tops," Zweig continues,

is their ill-founded reasoning: "Business looks good." It *always* looks good at the peaks. With prospects ripe for continued gains in earnings and dividends, investors optimistically lick their chops in anticipation of further market appreciation. But something goes astray. Business gets too overheated; the scramble for borrowed money to keep the boom rolling grows more intense, pressuring interest rates upward. The Federal Reserve, spotting increasing inflation, begins to tighten monetary growth, further exacerbating the surge in interest rates. Then, as short-term money instruments such as Treasury bills become more yield-attractive, the stock market begins to groan as the switching away from stocks accelerates, aided in no small part by the illiquidity in overly optimistic investors' portfolios [investors, that is, who have spent all their money on stocks already, and now have no more cash with which to buy any more]. Yet, most folks just continue holding their stocks—or worse, buying more— because "Business looks good." Finally, many months later it becomes apparent that business has slowed down . . . but it's too late for most investors. They've already been trapped by a crumbling stock market. "Optimism" gives way to "hope" that the business slowdown won't become a recession. But the drop in stock prices rocks consumer confidence, business dips some more and recession is reality. The stock market slump becomes a rout and investors' "hopes" are finally dashed. Seeing that a recession is in progress, investors "know" that earnings will slump; in "panic" they sell their stock, absorbing huge losses. Finally, all that selling, amid tons of pessimism, improves stock market liquidity [people once again have some cash], building a base for a new boom in the market, . . . one which *always* begins before business turns up.*

That's the cycle, all right, but it is easier to identify in hindsight than on any given Tuesday morning when you are trying to figure out which way business, and stocks, are headed. If in the early sixties you had held off investing while you waited for the next recession, you would have had to sit on the sidelines for six or eight years. "Business looked good"—and *was* good—for nearly a decade.

So for most people, the most practical, prudent alternative to trying to spot market tops and bottoms is to:

3. Diversify over time by not investing all at once. Spread your investments out to smooth the peaks and valleys of the market. Only, skip investing when the stock market averages are making new highs (or approaching old ones), and invest extraheavily in peri-

---

The Zweig Forecast, 747 Third Ave., New York, NY 10017.

ods when the averages are making new lows (or approaching old ones). The best times to invest are when the market has just taken a terrible dive of several days' or weeks' duration, and when talk of depression, the new bear market, and/or nuclear holocaust is rife. If the depression does come (and usually it does not), at least you will have been prudent enough to invest only money you didn't need to touch for years (Rule #1). And in the event of the holocaust, it wouldn't make much difference.

By investing more when the market is low and less when it is high, you will come out ahead when it is somewhere in between.

4. Diversify over several stocks in different industries. If all your money is riding on two or three stocks, you are exposed to much more risk than if you have diversified over a dozen or more. And, as stocks of companies within the same industry tend to move together, you will only be truly diversified if you choose from among different sectors of the economy.

5. And "diversify" in the same stock, by what's known as dollar-cost-averaging. To wit: If you are planning to buy 300 shares of a stock at $14, consider buying only 100 instead. Then if the stock never goes down and you never buy more, you can hardly complain. But if the natural ups and downs of life make the stock available some time later at, say, $12, you might then buy 100 or 200 shares more. It will be that much better a value.

Part of the theory here is that if you are in a terrible rush to buy the 300 shares, convinced that the stock is about to take off and there's not a minute to lose— you are very likely reacting to some hot news. And believe me, unless you are an insider trading (illegally) on privileged information, chances are you are one of the last to hear this hot news. Nine times out of ten you will be buying your shares from someone who heard it first. In which case, when the dust settles you may not regret having snagged only 100 shares instead of 300. If, on the other hand, you are not reacting to any particular news when you decide to purchase the stock, it is simply unlikely that the stock would go straight up without any dips from the day you buy it. And dips allow you to average down your cost.

Attracted by its 9% yield and hopelessly ignorant of its problems, I once bought 50 shares of Con Edison, Rock of Gibraltar, at 20. Shortly thereafter Con Ed omitted its quarterly dividend for the first time in twelve thousand years and, to my dismay, I found myself buying 100 more shares at 12. Then 100 more at 8½. Then, even, 100 more at 6. I kept buying because I just could not believe that the State of New York—which needed only to grant Con Ed's rate requests to solve all its problems—would prefer to have the company go bankrupt, and thus have to take on the burden of power generation itself. (Especially considering New York's own financial position at the time.) Sure enough, the state began cooperating, the dividend gradually was restored (even raised a notch), and the stock recovered to over 20. I would be lying if I told you I was smart enough to hold all 350 shares, or even most of them, all the way back up to 20. Dumb! But at least I held some. And I made sure that the first 50 shares I sold were the 50 I had purchased at 20, thus giving me a nice short-term capital loss to help out with my taxes. The last shares I sold I had held long enough to qualify for a long-term capital gain.

★ 6. A program of periodic investments in no-load mutual funds is for many people the most practical way to achieve diversification—let alone to avoid worrying about all this in the first place. (See Chapter 8.) However, if you *are* choosing your own stocks:

7. Don't invest in high-multiple stocks, even though they are the stocks of outstanding companies—and stocks which may, in the fullness of time, do extremely well. Their hefty multiples (price/earnings ratios) discount earnings growth far into the future. Which is to say that even if the growth comes in on schedule, the stocks may not go up. They're *already* up. And for most of us, it is hard to see that far into the future anyway. Should earnings not continue to grow as expected, such stocks can collapse, even though the underlying company may remain sound. What's more, it can hardly be argued that these stocks have been ignored and that they therefore represent some hidden value Wall Street has failed to discover.

8. Don't buy, either, stocks that "everyone" is recommending, regardless of the multiples at which they sell.

A few years back I attended the *Institutional Investor* conference—1,000 money managers representing billions upon billions of dollars. The men who really move the market. One of the panel sessions was devoted exclusively to ITT. The seminar organizer hadn't been able to find anyone bearish on the stock, so three of the panelists were bullish and the fourth volunteered to play the devil's advocate.

Well, when I heard their discussion, and saw all the heads nodding in the audience—at 1,000 shares a nod, I figured—I got this very guilty rush of adrenaline. What if I ran out of the room, rushed to the pay phone, and bought 50 shares? Would that be misuse of inside information? I decided it would not, and that's exactly what I did. At $44 a share. Any fool could see that at least a *few* of these men would do much the same thing after the meeting, or certainly when they got back to their desks. If they were not interested in ITT stock, why were they sitting through this seminar? And as there was no opposition meeting going on that I knew of persuading an equal number of people to rush to the phones and sell, I figured there would just have to be buying pressure on the stock. How could I miss?

The stock went straight down to 12.

Apparently, they had all put ITT in their portfolios and were now waiting for it to go up. But there was no one left to buy it. (I got out at 34 on the way down. What I *should* have done was buy the stock at 12, because it has since recovered.)

9. Choose instead bottom-tier stocks. Bottom-tier stocks can't fall out of favor—they are already out of favor.

10. Choose stocks that pay dividends at least equal to the going rate of interest on a daily savings account, but preferably a couple of points higher. These stocks will, necessarily, be selling at very low price/earnings ratios. They should be selling so low, and yielding such attractive dividends, not because they are in declining industries or because they have serious long-term problems (as some are and do), but simply because they have been ignored.

The companies you choose must not only pay handsome dividends, these dividends must be solid. You can never know for sure, of course, that a dividend won't be lowered or omitted, but you will be safest with companies that have been in business and paying dividends for many years; companies that have weathered a recession or two without cutting their dividend; companies whose earnings have generally been improving from year to year; companies with relatively little long-term debt; and companies whose dividends, although high, represent a relatively small portion of earnings in a typical year. A company that earns $1 a share and pays out 90 cents has much less room to maneuver than one that pays out 90 cents but earns $2.

If you cannot find such stocks, the market is probably too high. Stay away! Don't buy stocks just because you have money to burn, or because friends you know are talking about their profits. Wait.

The companies you choose may be in lackluster industries; or they may be in the midst of serious short-term *but temporary and surmountable* problems. When the problem first loomed, typically, "smart money" bailed out. Accordingly, the stock dropped sharply, then drifted lower for months as it became conventional wisdom not to buy such a dog—even though the price was now much lower and the problem, whatever it was, well on the way to solution.

Morse Shoe, a Boston-based shoe retailer, once sold as high as 34, when Wall Street was happy to pay 15 or 20 times earnings for a fine little growth company. Its earnings from 1964 to 1969 had been $1.10 a share, $1.54, $1.89, $2.13, $2.56, $2.85. A great trend-line.

Luckily I had never heard of Morse Shoe back then (although I had, sadly, heard of several others). The stock market turned sour, the longest business expansion in recent history came to an end, inflation began eating away at the country and raising interest rates and lowering bond and stock prices—and to top it all off, Morse Shoe's earnings began going in the wrong direction. The company operated leased shoe departments in chain stores around the country, and some of those chains, preferring to run the departments themselves, were giving Morse Shoe the boot.

I saw Morse Shoe for the first time, in 1973, in a list of stocks *Forbes* considered undervalued. The stock was around 2, down from 34, and earnings had dipped to 41 cents a share. According to *Forbes,* the company had a book value—the things it owned less the things it owed—of around $15 a share.

The stock was out of favor. What self-respecting institutional money manager was going to buy a stock, even for $2, whose earnings since 1969 had gone steadily down from $2.85 to 41 cents? What institution was even going to look at such a stock? Many retail brokerage houses, for their part, had arbitrary rules forbidding their reps to recommend—and in some cases even take orders for—stocks selling under $3 a share.

Yet the management of this company seemed sound, and was busily replacing lost outlets with new ones. People will probably always need shoes. In any case, the company had a net worth per share—things like cash and inventory—far in excess of its stock price. It even paid a 20-cent dividend (down from 75 cents), which on a $2 stock represented a 10% return. Still, few people would buy it. Who cared about Morse Shoe at 2 when the world was about to end? Who cared about Morse Shoe at 2 when you could buy IBM at 160?

As it happened the world did not end, Morse Shoe's earnings rebounded to $2.78 by 1976, the dividend was raised to 50 cents, and by the time the stock got up near 12 an institution or two began considering it for its portfolio.

Granted, the market may never again present such opportunities. It was tremendously oversold in those bleak days of 1974 and 1975. But even if this is an extreme case, it is an example of how profitable it can be to seek out value. By 1978 the stock had increased more than tenfold and still, as of this writing, sells around 6 times earnings. For IBM to have done as well it would have had to go from 160 to 1600.

Note that throughout all this Morse Shoe was a good little *company,* despite its difficulties. But at 34 Morse Shoe was an awful *stock* (selling at a high p/e, at more than 3 times book value, and paying a 2% dividend); while at 2 it was a terrific stock (selling at 5 times depressed earnings, less than one-sixth book value, and paying a 10% dividend).

Why invest in companies nobody's ever heard of when you can invest in General Motors, Sears, Xerox, or Kodak? Why not the best? For one thing, you pay a premium for this peace of mind. But also, the peace of mind you get is at least partly illusory. True, these companies are financially impregnable. But their stocks can go down almost as much as any other. General Motors was $113 a share in 1965, $29 nine years later. (By late 1978 it had climbed about halfway back up.) Xerox sold at $171 in 1972; it had dropped to $46 five years later.

11. Beware the deceptive p/e. The price/earnings ratio is the guide most investors use to get a quick fix on a stock. It is listed in the paper every day. The p/e tells you how much p (price) you have to pay for $1 of this wallet's e (earnings).

However, the best the newspaper can do is calculate the p/e based on that day's price and *last year's* earnings. What you are buying is the right to share in next year's and future years' earnings.

Chrysler, which had a terrific 1976 and earned $5.45 a share (of which just 30 cents was actually paid out to shareholders), was recently selling at 16½—3 times earnings. *Chrysler,* for God's sake. The thing to note is that the auto industry, like construction or any other industry whose profits rise and fall with the economy, is cyclical—Chrysler, even more so. The year before Chrysler earned $5.45, it lost $4.71 (and there were those who wondered how long the company would survive). IBM, by way of contrast, *never* loses money; it just grows and grows. So Chrysler is selling at 3 times earnings . . . sort of.

Actually, the stock might prove to be a good bet at 16½. Certainly it is a better buy today at 16½ than it was in 1968, at 72, although not as good as in 1975, when it sold for just 7½. At 16½ there were as many people betting that it would go up as that it would go down—that's the price at which supply and demand for the stock currently meet. If you look in this morning's paper you can see which bettors turned out to be right. If the stock has gone up since this writing, you can be sure it did so not because it was selling at a low multiple of last year's earnings, but because it was selling at a low multiple of what people expect future earnings will be.

Now take the opposite case. Zayre, a billion-dollar discount chain, was once a high-flying growth company selling for $47 a share. It earned around $2 a share in 1971, 1972, and 1973. In 1974 earnings dropped in the recession to a mere 14 cents. At $5 a share, the stock was listed in the paper as selling for 36 times earnings, seemingly an outrageously high multiple. Yet "book value" was over $20 a share, and there was the hope that if the economy ever recovered, and Zayre with it, the company might return to its $2-a-share earnings level, and perhaps even continue its stalled growth. Seen in that light, $5 a share was more like 2½ times earnings than 36 times.

Thus in choosing stocks it is necessary to keep the p/e figure in perspective, to take an average of the last *several* years' earnings, and to think more in terms of the future than the past. This is particularly true with companies—autos, cement, construction, paper, and many others—whose profits rise and fall in cycles.

As it turned out, Zayre earned nearly $1 in 1975 and over $2 in 1976. (W. T. Grant, on the other hand, an even larger retailer, went bankrupt. Not all failing companies recover.)

12. Never buy a stock you think is fairly valued. Never even buy one you think should, by rights, be selling 10% or 15% higher. Always wait for one you are convinced is selling *way beneath* its fair value. Judging by its book value it should be selling much higher; judging by its future earnings potential it should be selling much higher. But it isn't. Why pay a "fair" price for a stock like AT&T—which is to say, a "full" price—when so many others sell for much less? When a stock is fairly—fully—priced, there is sizable potential for loss if something goes wrong, only moderate potential for gain if things continue to go right. If the only stocks you can find seem reasonably priced, wait. When they have fallen by 20% or 40% they will look much better.

Try to find companies that not only pay large secure dividends but which seem to be able also to pass on inflation to their customers and to grow in real terms. There shouldn't *be* such companies selling for 5 or 10 times earnings; but, at least since the early seventies and as of this writing, there are. Lots of them. Brokers will be delighted to help you find them and to supply you with information, but you might be just as well served letting *Forbes* find them for you and saving a good portion of the brokerage fees.

Forbes, more than *Business Week* or *Fortune,* is written for the investor rather than the businessman. The editors of the magazine have always stressed a level-headed, value-oriented approach to investing.

They frequently run stories on companies, or whole lists of companies, that seem to be undervalued. This doesn't mean *Forbes* is always right, by any means—or even that when they are right the stock market "agrees." But for $21 a year, you get the services of several dozen financially sophisticated editors, writers, and columnists.

13. Don't waste money subscribing to investment letters or expensive services. The more expensive investor newsletters and computer services only make sense for investors with lots of money—if then. Besides their (admittedly tax-deductible) cost there is the problem that they are liable to tempt you into buying and scare you into selling much too often, thereby incurring much higher brokerage fees and capital gains taxes than you otherwise might. There is the added problem that half the experts, at any given time, are likely to be wrong. (Indeed, there is one letter which simply analyzes the sentiment of all the others—and advises you do the opposite, on the not-unreasonable theory that when most of the services are bullish, it's time to sell, and vice versa.)

On May 27, 1977, Dr. Martin Zweig issued a special bulletin to his $95-a-year subscribers. "A *Bear Market* is now underway," his bulletin began. "Sell *EVERYTHING.*"

Three weeks later, *Smart Money* issued a special bulletin to *its* $50-a-year subscribers. (The market, meanwhile, had moved *up* 2 or 3 percent.) Having the previous month recommended Twentieth Century-Fox at 11¼, and having seen it run straight to 22 (on the strength of *Star Wars*), *Smart Money* was in an ebullient mood. "This could well be an *outstanding buying opportunity,"* the bulletin began. "The ingredients are there for a significant upward move (100 points). New all time highs are not out of the question.

As usual, we'd like to factor in as many pertinent investment considerations as possible. They're all screaming *buy!*"

The market dropped 100 points.

For months Zweig had been bearish on the market —with some justification—while *Smart Money*—also with some justification—had been bullish.

I have a friend whose market report is highly sophisticated and, at $3,000 or so a year (12 issues), is aimed at big money managers. Lots of big money managers probably don't understand half of what my friend writes in these reports—he's that sophisticated (and his sentences defy punctuation)—but they send commission dollars his way in order to get it, anyway. Many probably read just the first and last paragraphs, which summarize the broad outlook for the market and suggest broad strategy for these institutional money managers. He is one of the smartest, most thoughtful, best-read men I have ever met. Sometimes he's right; sometimes he's wrong.

You want to know my idea of real market brilliance? A well-heeled former associate editor of *Fortune,* now back in the business world, sold all his stocks in March of 1977, the day before the market began a rapid 100-point slide. It was pure genius. I was green with envy and admiration.

"Peter, how did you *know?*" I asked him, making a mental note to pay better heed to his opinions in the future.

"I needed the cash to buy my apartment," he said.

Had he been in a position to profit by selling me his market savvy, like a broker or investment advisor, he might not have been so forthright.

(Nor as it turned out was the timing so brilliant, after all. One of his major holdings was Twentieth Century-Fox. Had he held on a little longer, until the release of *Star Wars,* he would have more than doubled his money, despite the falling market.)

You can tell a lot about most publicly traded companies just by obtaining the current issue of the Standard & Poor's monthly *Stock Guide*. Many brokers give them to their clients free.

This little booklet provides key facts about almost any company you are likely to invest in: its ticker symbol; where it's traded; how many institutions own a piece; how much they own; what business the company is in; what the stock has done over the last fifteen years or so; the price/earnings ratio; dividend yield; how long a dividend has been paid; and some sketchy balance-sheet and earnings figures. One column even gives letter grades to the quality of the company's growth and stability of its earnings and dividends.

Standard & Poor's is hardly infallible, but they are probably as good at this as you or most brokers are, so there is something to be said for letting them do all the work. Any company rated B+ or better should certainly be sound enough to qualify for the kind of portfolio I'm suggesting, at least on the basis of its past performance. You should not write off companies rated B or even B—, either, particularly if you have some reason to think their prospects are bright.

You could spend many hours writing for past annual reports, reading footnotes, consulting your accountant, even visiting the company and testing its products—but much of what you will ever know about a company you can find out in 60 seconds with the *Stock Guide*.

In three minutes more you can read the one-page summary sheet Standard & Poor's puts out on just about every public company. Brokers happily drop these sheets in the mail, if asked, or you may be able to locate them at the library. These minianalyses, while not tremendously astute, pack in a lot of relevant information.

There is one widely read investment service that *has* been shown consistently to beat the market. The weekly *Value Line Survey,* at $285 a year (tax-deductible), ranks 1,650 stocks from 1 to 5, with Group 1 expected to do best over the coming year and Group 5 worst. Remarkably, in each of the last dozen years the rankings have performed in almost exactly the order they were supposed to. In an up year, Group 1 stocks rose more, on average, than those in the lower groups, with Group 5 stocks rising least; in down years, Group 1 stocks, on average, fell the least. Unfortunately, after taking into consideration brokerage commissions, taxes—and the chance Value Line will not work as well in the future as it has in the past—this service is not a sure way to riches. But its record is nonetheless remarkable.

Write Arnold Bernhard & Co., 5 East 44th Street, New York, NY 10017 for more information. There is generally a $29 10-week trial offer for new subscribers, and that includes a book with a full page of information on each of the 1,650 stocks in the survey. If Value Line were ever expanded to even more than 1,650 stocks, it could be even more valuable: as I have argued, many of the best values are among the least-followed stocks. (Well over 3,000 different issues are quoted in the *Wall Street Journal* each day.)

★ 14. **However you choose them, once you have selected 10 or 20 high-yielding, low-p/e stocks—not all at once, remember, diversified over time—sit back and relax.** If the stocks go down, you are still getting as much in dividends as you would be getting in interest from a savings bank. But as long as the dividends seem secure, it is unlikely the stocks will decline too disastrously: the more the stocks fall, the more attractive their dividends become to prospective buyers. The dividends should serve to cushion market declines somewhat. And if you have managed to buy these stocks under the auspices of a Keogh Plan (see Chapter 4), the dividends will be accumulating tax-free.

Over the long run, unless you have chosen companies that are fundamentally unsound, it is likely that each of the stocks will at one time or another be worth a good deal more than you paid for it. This will happen either because of nothing more than the simple ups and downs of the economy and of the stock market and of your stock in particular; or because profits and/ or the dividend have increased—if only in step with inflation; or, if you are really lucky, because your company gets caught up in some new financial fad (as with an insulation company around the time of the energy conservation crunch), or becomes the target of some other company's takeover bid (which, at the rate profitable or asset-rich little companies are being taken over these days, is not so farfetched).

15. Invest—don't speculate. It's one thing to take risks in low-priced stocks that you hope, over time, may work out their problems and triple in value. If you can afford the risk, it may reward you handsomely.

It's quite another to jump in and out of stocks (or options or commodities), hoping to "play the market" successfully. Every time you jump, your broker cuts down your stake. Jump once a month for a year (and to the speculator a month seems an eternity), and you have transferred half your stake to your broker. Even jumping once a year is likely to cost you about as much in commissions as you would receive in dividends.

Why it costs $110 to buy and sell 200 shares of a

$10 stock (what—do they do it one share at a time?) when it costs just a dime to clear a check, or $25 to prepare an entire tax return, no one knows. But as long as it does, investors of modest means cannot afford to do anything but "buy and hold," unless they are awfully confident they know which way individual stocks, and the market as a whole, are headed. Winning some and losing some just won't do when you have to fork over 5% to the dealer for each hand.

Buy value and hold it. Don't switch in and out; don't try to outsmart the market.

16. Sell only when a stock has gone up so much that you feel it no longer represents a good value. Don't sell because you think business or the market generally is going to get bad, because

● if you think so, chances are lots of other people think so, too, and the market may already have discounted this possibility (that is, the stock price may already reflect it);

● you could be wrong;

● even if business does get bad, someday it will get better—and in the meantime you are collecting dividends rather than paying brokerage commissions and capital gains taxes.

There are one drawback and three basic risks in following the strategy of buying high-yielding low-p/e stocks outlined above.

The drawback: For people in very high tax brackets who can't invest through a tax-deferred retirement plan of some sort, half or more of those high dividends go straight to the government. Such individuals may reasonably decide to forgo the dividend "cushion" and seek low-p/e stocks that reinvest most or all their earnings, thus deferring taxes and adding to the potential for capital gains appreciation instead of dividends.*

Risk number 1: Your choice of stocks will be so egregious, or business in general so bad, that each will, in turn, cut or even eliminate its dividend and your stocks will dip, fall, plummet, or even disappear altogether.

Risk number 2: Long-term interest rates, already high by historical standards, will move substantially higher, and stay there, rendering those fat dividends of yours that much less attractive, and providing that much less cushion. (Of course, were this the case, any other stocks you had bought—or bonds, for that matter —would in all likelihood decline about as badly.)

Risk number 3: After six to eight weeks of following this strategy, of watching your stocks go nowhere except maybe to edge down a little, and of receiving one dividend check for $11 that doesn't quite pay for half a tank of gas, you will become itchy, you will remind yourself that you only live once, you will hear stories about the man over in personnel who turned $2,000 into $17,000 in soybeans in a month—and, feeling bad about having given your broker so little business with this new buy-and-hold strategy of yours, you will call him and ask that he sell you out at a small loss (made no less small by the commissions). Then you will take your money and invest in something fun!

That's the thing. There is a thin line between "investing" and "playing the market"; it is a line that takes great self-discipline to draw; and it is a line that makes all the financial difference in the world.

---

*It is ironic that in the early seventies the bank trust departments, which went so heavily into the low-dividend glamour stocks for their massive pension fund accounts, had nothing to gain for their clients by going after capital gains instead of dividends. Pension funds are not taxed, and so it was particularly irresponsible for the trust department managers to ignore dividends as they did.

CHAPTER 6

Choosing (to Ignore) Your Broker

> What always impresses me is how much better the relaxed, long-term owners of stocks do with their portfolios than the traders do with their switching of inventory. The relaxed investor is usually better informed and more understanding of essential values; he is more patient and less emotional; he pays smaller annual capital gains taxes; he does not incur unnecessary brokerage commissions; and he avoids behaving like Cassius by "thinking too much."
>
> —Lucien O. Hooper, *Forbes* columnist

Wait a minute (you say). You've told me all this but you haven't told me the part about choosing a brilliant but level-headed, highly experienced, and highly ethical broker. Where's the part about him? If I can find a guy who knows how to make money in the market, and who spends all day at it, why do I have to know about anything but how to retire?

There is a bit in a Woody Allen movie where Woody is standing in line, and a man behind him is lecturing his date, loudly and pretentiously, about Marshall McLuhan. Finally, Woody turns and says (in effect): "I don't know why you're talking so loud, but since you are I have to tell you I think you've got McLuhan all wrong." "Oh, yeah?" says the other man. "Well, I just happen to *teach a course* on McLuhan at Columbia." "Well, that's funny," says Allen, unfazed, "because *I* just happen to have McLuhan right here." Whereupon he goes behind a prop and pulls out

Marshall McLuhan. McLuhan looks at the man and says dryly: "You know nothing of my work. How you ever got to teach a course in anything is totally amazing."

Woody Allen looks straight into the camera, at us, and says: "Boy, if life were only like this!"

Indeed. I have terrible news about brokers and money managers generally—news which I expect you've suspected, but couldn't quite believe, all along. There *are* no brokers who can beat the market consistently and by enough of a margin to more than make up for their brokerage fees. Or if there are a few, they are not going to work for peanuts—and any account under $100,000 is peanuts. Or if they will—because they are just starting out in the business or have a soft spot in their heart for you—*there's no way for you to know who they are.* Even if they can prove to you that they have done very well in the past (not just say it—prove it), that doesn't mean they will do very well in the future.

If you get 256 people into a room and give them each a coin to flip, the odds are that half of them—128—will flip heads on the first try. That is the object, you tell them: to flip heads. Of those 128 winners, 64 will flip heads on the next go-round as well. Twice running. Not bad. Thirty-two people will flip heads three times in a row, sixteen people will flip heads four times in a row, eight will flip heads five times in a row, four will succeed six times in a row, two will rack up an incredible seven straight successes, and one— one out of all 256 in the crowd—will flip heads eight times in a row. What talent! What genius!

What nonsense. This man is no more or less likely than anyone else in the room to flip heads the ninth time. His chances are fifty-fifty. He is not a genius, he is a statistic in a probability formula. As is some other

man in the crowd of 256 (who may actually *be* a
genius) who, odds are, failed eight times running to
flip heads.

In any given year, half the stock market players will
beat the averages and half will do worse.* After eight
years, one player out of every 256—be he broker or
mutual fund, private investor or bank trust department
—is likely to have done better than average *every
single year.* (Except that, since we all want to put our
best feat forward, chances are that more than one will
say he did.)

That player, naturally, will attract quite a following.
What talent! What genius!

What nonsense.

I'm not saying the stock market is *all* luck. Never-
theless, it is enough of a crap shoot that luck has a
great deal more to do with it than any professional
money man is going to want to admit.

By and large you should manage your own money.
No one is going to care about it as much as you. And
no one but you is going to manage it for free.

This runs very much against the accepted line. The
accepted line is that your money is too important to be
managed in your spare time: you should let a full-
time professional manage it for you even though you
will have to pay him to do so.

Who are these professionals and how well do they do
and what do they charge? How do you find one who
has been right eight times running—and *are* his chances
any better than anyone else's to be right the ninth
time?

I am being driven from a Boston TV station to
Harvard Business School by a fellow alumnus, an in-

---

*Actually, more than half will do worse because players pay brokerage
commissions, stock market averages don't.

vestment counselor with an outstanding firm. He is paid not to manage money or to make trades, but, rather, to advise people on how to invest. He was just on television giving his expert financial opinion. (Utilities looked good, he said.) He came on right after 1976 independent presidential candidate Eugene McCarthy, and is on this show periodically giving his views.

His views are not what you would call profound. Before he goes on the air I see him reading another company's views. And those views, in part, would have come from a compilation of other people's views.

In any case, in the car after the show, he is telling me that he doesn't believe "little money," in all candor, *can* beat the averages. He considers $100,000 or less little money. He does think big money can—but he can't say for sure.

"My biggest pitch," he says, "is so simple really—it's that clients shouldn't put all their eggs in one basket. I know that sounds like plain common sense you'd learn in the third grade, it's real simple, but that's what I'm paid to advise." He is paid $40,000 or $50,000 a year; his services are billed out to clients at two or three times that price. He advises Big Money. He recommends utilities on TV *after* they've doubled in price (maybe they'll double again?). Welcome to the world of professional money management.

Item: On June 30, 1967, the publisher, editor-in-chief, and editor of *Forbes* magazine mounted the *New York Times* stock pages on the wall. They threw ten darts apiece, tried again with the darts that missed the pages altogether, and invested a hypothetical $1,000 in each dart-selected stock. Ten years later, the portfolio had appreciated by 50%. Over the same period the Dow Jones industrial average had risen only 6.5%; the Standard & Poor's 500, just 11%. And most money managers hadn't done even that well.

Item: Computer Directions Advisors, Inc., a Maryland financial consulting firm, programmed a computer to choose 100 different portfolios of 25 stocks apiece —*at random*—from the 2,700-odd stocks on the New York and American Stock Exchanges. *Eighty-two* of the 100 randomly selected portfolios did better than the S&P 500 over the ten years from 1967 to 1976. Ninety-nine of them beat the S&P 500 in 1976. Concluded *Money* magazine: "These results suggest that it pays to look—as the computer did—beyond the large, intensively analyzed companies in the S&P 500."

Item: On February 28, 1977, the *Wall Street Journal* reported that, "judging by the results of the pooled investment funds banks and insurance companies run, more than three-fourths of the professional managers failed to do as well as the market averages over the past two years. In fact, fewer than one-fourth of them have achieved results as good as or better than the averages, whether for the past year, the past two years or the past four or eight years."

Only 13 of 85 major bank-managed mutual funds did better than the Standard & Poor's 500 from 1970 to 1975. Just 12 of 171 mutual funds monitored by *Barron's* beat the market in 1975 (although in 1977 the funds were doing better).

It's not that professional money managers are dumber than average, or lazier than average—just that the market averages don't have to pay brokerage commissions or advisory fees, and so generally outperform people, or institutions, which do.

What is more significant is that among money managers there are exceedingly few who consistently do substantially better than their fellows (or substantially worse). This year's winners may be next year's losers.

In school you can pretty well assume that an A-student this year is likely to do well next year. Not so among money managers. They will flip heads a few years in a row . . . but they are just about as likely to flip tails the next. On Wall Street, it is not enough to be smart and hard-working. There are a great many smart, hard-working people on Wall Street. Smart is taken for granted. Lucky is the way to get rich. (The other way used to be to be a broker.) Inside information doesn't hurt, either.

As for the not-inconsiderable number of dumb people on Wall Street (and in "Wall Street" I include the entire network of electronic tributaries flowing from all over the world into the mighty Manhattan delta), their existence is undeniable. Which naturally gives rise to the question, If They're So Dumb, How Come They're Still in Business? But this just proves my point: Investment success has at least as much to do with luck, patience, psychological balance (unconflicted greed, for example, versus unrelenting guilt and masochism), and inside information (you don't have to be a genius to be well-connected) as it does with intelligence.

In fact, recognizing the virtual futility of trying to beat the averages, quite a few money managers have gone so far as to invest in "index funds"—funds that mirror the stock market averages, and which therefore cannot fail to do as well once the initial brokerage fee is paid. Such money managers thereby abdicate any responsibility to search out the best values; and they ignore, by definition, the thousands of publicly traded stocks which are not among the 30 Dow Jones industrials or the Standard & Poor's 500. But they are assured of not doing any worse than "average."

It is a cop-out, but it does speak eloquently to the frustration financial professionals have felt in trying to choose "winning" portfolios . . . and it does emphasize the way in which professional money managers will concentrate their investments among the 500 major stocks, whether the thousands that remain are good values or not.

If the professionals do no better than darts—and there is a lot of reason to believe they do not—then how much is it worth to have them manage your money?

The answer is that you are probably best off minimizing your "overhead"—paying as little as possible in brokerage and advisory fees. But before we get to discount brokers, it's worth spending some time discussing a theory that has caused much wringing of hands on Wall Street. It is called *random walk,* and to the extent it is valid it helps to explain why professionals are just as apt to blunder as you or I. That is, after all, an intuitively unpalatable notion.

The random walk theory holds that you cannot predict the price of a stock by looking back at charts that show where it has been ("technical analysis"), nor by studying the prospects of the company whose stock it is ("fundamental analysis"). On any given day, a stock —or the market as a whole—is as likely to go up as down.

The reason, according to this theory, is that the stock market is "efficient." As soon as a new bit of information becomes known about a company (or the world), it is reflected almost immediately in the price of the stock (or the market). By the time that bit of information filters down to you or me or much of anyone else, it is already reflected in the price of the stock. It has been "discounted."

True, if you happen to be the daughter of the judge who is presiding over a $900 million antitrust suit brought by a tiny computer firm against IBM, and if no one on Wall Street is taking the suit at all seriously, but your daddy has just told you he's going to surprise the pants off those bastards at IBM and award the full $900 million to the little computer company . . . well, then you could probably profit quite handsomely by buying stock in the little computer company. (You could also get yourself and your daddy into very hot water.) You have "inside information."

But, inside information apart (and believe me, if you're hearing it from your broker or the company's sales manager's brother-in-law, it's no longer inside information—everyone and his brother has heard it), the market, according to the random walk theory, efficiently digests all the information available to it.

Thus when a company announces higher earnings, the stock may go up—or it may sit pat or even decline. It depends how those higher earnings compare with what the market was expecting. It's not enough to buy U.S. Steel thinking that, with an upturn in the economy, steel profits will be good. If *you* think that, chances are lots of other people have already thought so, too, and the possibility is already reflected in the price. Only if the gain proves more than expected will the price rise.

So you not only have to know what steel profits will be—you also have to try to figure out how that compares with what other people expect. Which gives you not just one, but two chances to guess wrong. Between 1968 and 1977 IBM profits tripled and its dividend quintupled. Yet a share of IBM in November 1977 was actually worth less than in September 1968.

Choosing a horse, you just have to guess which one will run the fastest. With a stock, you have to guess how well a company will do; whether that will make the stock go up or down; and which way the track itself (the market) is moving. (The advantage in owning a stock is that the race doesn't end. You don't have to sell the stock until you want to . . . you *own* something. If you have chosen a good value, you will receive dividends, share in future growth, and with any luck, ultimately be vindicated.)

The random walk theory naturally is anathema to

the men and women whose livelihoods and self-esteem depend on convincing clients they know which way stock prices will go. Many studies have been undertaken to refute it. It is in connection with these studies that computers are made to simulate dart-throwing monkeys. Yet the evidence is that anyone who *can* regularly beat the averages to any meaningful degree is an exceptionally rare individual.

Burton Malkiel, a professor at Princeton drafted by President Ford to sit on the three-man Council of Economic Advisers, wrote an excellent stock market guide called *A Random Walk Down Wall Street.* In it he makes a tight case for random walk, citing numerous rigorously designed and executed studies. Yet he remains himself "a random walker with a crutch." He argues that random walk theory does not have to be absolutely right or wrong. It is *largely* right. It is *largely* true that you can't outguess the market. And it is particularly difficult to outguess the market by enough to justify the brokerage commissions you will incur by switching in and out.

David Dreman, author of *Psychology and the Stock Market,* writing in *Barron's,* made a good case *against* random walk. He pointed out that stock markets have always been irrational—à la Avon at 60 times earnings—and concluded that a rational man could therefore outdo the herd. "Market history gives cold comfort to the Random Walkers," he writes. " 'Rational' investors in France, back in 1719, valued the Mississippi Company at 80 times all the gold and silver in the country—and, just a few months later, at only a pittance."

It is true, I think, that by keeping one's head and sticking to value, one may do better than average. But it's not easy. Because the question is not so much whether the market is rational as whether by being rational we can beat it. Had Dreman been alive in

1719, he might very reasonably have concluded that the Mississippi Company was absurdly overpriced at, say, three times all the gold and silver in France. And he might have shorted some.* At six times all the gold and silver in France he might have shorted more. At twenty times all the gold and silver in France he might have been ever-so-rational—and thoroughly ruined. It would have been cold comfort to hear through the bars of debtors' prison that, some months later, rationality had at last prevailed. A driveling imbecile, on the other hand, caught up in the crowd's madness, might have ridden the stock from three times to eighty times all the gold and silver in France, and, quite irrationally, struck it rich.

There *are* rare individuals who can consistently do significantly better than the market. One—as of this writing, at least—is the pony-tailed president of the Unicorn Group, a money management firm, Walter Peters. In six of the past eight years, the funds under his management have performed better than 99% of the more than 4,000 pools of money monitored by A. G. Becker & Co.

Peters relies on an international network of 18 outstanding specialists in politics, economics and finance —not to pick stocks, but to discern crucial world trends. He is a modern-day Rothschild with 18 "sons" (most of them older than he is) feeding him information.

There is no guarantee that Peters will continue to outperform most money managers, but if you have $1 million, his minimum account, you might give him a call. (On the other hand, it is just when a money manager becomes a star on the financial pages, as Peters most deservedly has, that his peak may have passed.

---

*See page 127 for an explanation of short-selling.

If nothing else, all the celebrity may affect the delicate psychological and judgmental balance that led to the success in the first place.)

Another man who could have made you rich is John Marks Templeton, a fervently but eclectically religious former Rhodes scholar who has managed to beat the Dow by an average of 8% a year since the thirties. Unfortunately, he cannot live forever. A dollar invested in the Templeton Growth Fund in 1954 is worth around $15 today. "Because John felt that God was with him," one associate asserts, "he invested with incredible boldness. The results make me think maybe he's right—maybe God is with him." Even more instrumental in his success than the Lord, however, may have been his relentless insistence on value, wherever he had to go to find it. He bought European stocks after World War II, convinced that the Marshall Plan would cause business abroad to boom. At one time fully three-fourths of his fund was invested in Japanese stocks, because stocks there were selling at much lower price/earnings ratios than stocks in the United States. When those p/e's rose dramatically, Templeton shifted his equally dramatic profits to countries offering better values.

Templeton shuns growth stocks selling for twenty times earnings and finds smaller, unrecognized companies—in some cases growing equally fast—selling at four or eight times earnings.

It takes special initiative to do what no one else is doing. More than that, it's *lonely*. That, I suspect, is where God fits in.

Successes like Walter Peters and John Marks Templeton poke big holes in the random walk theory, however valid it may be for most investors buying and selling widely followed stocks.

Unfortunately, choosing a winning investment advisor, even if you can afford his services,* is not much easier than choosing a winning stock.

Choosing a winning *broker* will be even harder. Unlike an investment advisor, a broker spends much of his time on the phone selling to new clients, selling to old clients, giving stock quotes and up-to-the-moment market appraisals, talking sports, talking politics, making excuses for recommendations that have gone sour—or handling paperwork, seeing that trades get made, and straightening out back-office snafus. He has little time to search out exceptional values or to formulate broad economic and financial views, as investment advisors and money managers theoretically do.

And unlike an investment advisor, who takes a set annual fee for his services, a broker only makes money when you trade in or out of a stock. Eager as a broker may be to see your account prosper, that is not his first interest. With rare exceptions (and all brokers will claim to be that rare exception), his first interest is to do well himself. His first interest is commissions to feed his family. His first interest is hitting the bonus level at the end of the month that will pay for his family's trip to Disney World. He is as anxious as any automobile salesman that you be pleased with the car you buy—more so, because the better you do, the more business you are likely to give him in the future—but his first interest is to sell you the car. He will never tell you this, but you should never forget it.

Which reminds me:

17. Never buy anything from a broker who calls you up cold. This is so basic as not to warrant elaboration.

---

*Generally ¾ to 1% of the total assets under management. This fee, unlike brokerage commissions, is tax-deductible. Most good investment counselors will not take on accounts of less than $100,000—it's not worth their time.

If most brokers are wrong as often as they are right —and they are—if the market is *largely* a random walk and if the *Stock Guide, Forbes,* and the *Wall Street Journal* are likely to do as well for you as a team of personal advisors—at a tiny fraction of the price—then why do you need a broker at all?

You need him to execute your trades, to give you stock quotes, to allow you to buy stocks on margin, to hold your certificates, to mail you your dividend checks and monthly statements and annual reports—*and all these services are available from "discount brokers" at discounts ranging up to 75%.* What they will not do is hold your hand, give you bad advice (or good), or, most important, try to sell you anything.

A discount broker won't call you in the middle of the day—in the middle of a root canal, if you are a dentist—to tell you the bad news that's just come over the tape about one of your stocks.

But that's good.

Had he called, you might have panicked into selling. In so many cases, seemingly dreadful news turns out to be news everyone expected, or news about a Brazilian subsidiary that accounts for 3% of the company's sales, or news that pales beside the good news that will be announced the following week. If it's *really* important news, and no one expected it, the stock will be shut down from trading before you can sell, anyway, and when it reopens, sharply lower, the new price will reflect investors' assessment of the news.

With a discount broker, you won't rush into making unnecessary trades. You can finish the root canal in peace.

There is an old joke on Wall Street. "Well," the joke goes, "the broker made money and the firm made money—and two out of three ain't bad." I have heard this joke, often, from a broker with an unobstructed view of the Statue of Liberty and a number of important institutional accounts. One of these accounts entrusted his firm with $175,000 for a flier in options. The institution was shrewd in its timing, as it turned out. The stock market rallied dramatically. Never could one have made as much in options as then. Yet in two months, through an elaborate series of computer-assisted ins, outs, and straddles, the firm's options trader managed to turn that $175,000 into $10,000—generating $87,000 in commissions along the way.

Anyway, if you already are "in the market," making occasional trades, my first suggestion—if you can bear to do it—is that you go through last year's confirmation slips to see what you paid in commissions. You may be surprised. I didn't know I churned my own account, either. Next to rent, it turned out that brokerage commissions were my biggest expense in life.

Adding up one's commissions is a calculation rarely performed. Computerized monthly brokerage statements leave the figure tactfully untallied. For tax purposes, the commission is just lumped in as part of the cost of purchasing a stock, or lumped out as a diminution of the receipts from selling one. (It wouldn't be so bad if the IRS would let us treat the things as the deductible business expenses they clearly are.)

If it turns out you didn't spend much on brokerage commissions last year, fine. But if you are unpleasantly surprised, as I was, I have another suggestion. Not a silly suggestion like "stop churning your account"—a practical suggestion that allows you to enjoy your little vice for less. Switch your account to a discount broker.

Depending on your relationship with your current broker, this may be easier said than done. My own full-price broker is probably the best in his mid-Manhattan office. The brightest, the most personable, the busiest. Our typical phone conversation goes like this:

VOICE: Mr. ———'s office.

(Already this is ridiculous because he has neither an office nor a secretary, so this just means both his hands have phones in them and he can't pick up a third.)

ME (*playing along*): Is Mr. ——— in?

VOICE: One moment, please.

HIM: Hello?

ME: Who was that who answered the ph—

HIM: Can you hold on a minute?

(All I want to know is one stock quote, but I want to know it badly enough to hold on.)

HIM: Hi.

ME: Hi. How am I doing?

HIM: Fine, thanks, how are *you*?

ME: Fine. How's my stock?

HIM: Not very . . . can you hold on a minute?

(*Silence*)

(I should really just wait for the evening paper, but because stock quotes are free and an easy way to avoid concentrating on what I'm supposed to be concentrating on, I hold on.)

HIM: Can you believe that guy? He's short 500 Xerox and . . .

Eventually I get my quote, but it takes some doing. Getting a whole list of quotes can be like sitting through a soap opera waiting for the plot tidbits. To keep me listening, once in a while he throws me a quote.

The problem is, we've become friends. Because we're friends I resent it if he's busy when I call. And because I work for a living, I resent it if I'm busy when *he* calls. What's ludicrous is that, because we're friends, he resents it if *I'm* busy when *he* calls. (I installed a special phone, just for him, with a bell I could turn off when I didn't want to be interrupted; but he soon caught on and started calling on the other line, which I had to keep open for business calls.)

So it boils down to this: I wouldn't drop my broker

any more than I'd drop any other good friend. And this costs me a small fortune. Three such friends and I'd be out on the street.

I'm paying him to listen to my troubles, and I am paying to listen to his troubles. The fact is, I think my troubles are more interesting than his, and I think my investment advice is as good—so why isn't he paying me? We have often discussed that very point, and he couldn't agree with me more, and I keep paying him (although I now deal with a discount broker as well).

18. Minimize your transaction costs. Unless yours has consistently outperformed the market, in which case you won't believe any of this anyway, you should shop around for the cheapest broker. You will save hundreds or thousands of dollars in commissions and lose little or nothing.

Many of the discounters have branch offices around the country and toll-free numbers you can call if you are out-of-state. (See pages 178–9.) I repeat: Most perform all the services of a regular broker, minus the advice and the chitchat. Full-rate brokers will claim that they provide better executions on trades—that they get you better prices than discount brokers can. However, there is no evidence that this is true, and, on small trades particularly, it is most unlikely.

The only real drawback is the minimum commission most charge of $25 or $30 per trade. If you are a really small investor, buying $1,000 worth of stock at a time, or even less, that's what you will pay, coming and going—and that's no discount. (Regular brokers have similar minimums, so it's no premium either).

So Why Not Hire a Monkey?

Does all this mean a monkey could handle your financial planning? No. It takes intelligence to match your financial strategy with your circumstances: how much risk you can afford, what time horizons you are looking at, what tax bracket you are in. It takes intelligence to try to perceive value. A monkey might buy municipal bonds for a Keogh Plan—but that's like throwing money out the window. A monkey might buy growth stocks for an eighty-year-old widow who needs a secure income. A monkey might buy Avon instead of Ford, as the Morgan Guaranty Trust Company, and others, did.

A monkey does not have what investing well really takes: common sense.

CHAPTER 7

Hot Tips, Inside Information—
and Other Fine Points

> If you bet on a horse, that's gambling. If you bet
> you can make three spades, that's entertainment.
> If you bet cotton will go up three points, that's
> business. See the difference?
> —Blackie Sherrode (as quoted
> by James Dines in *Technical Analysis*)

Hot Tips

Here is what to do with hot tips. If you get a hot
tip, make a note of it and pretend to be very interested. But don't buy. If the thing takes off, listen a little more closely the next time this fellow has a tip. If it
gets mauled, look bitter the next time you see him. He
will assume that you bought the stock; he will feel
guilty; and he will buy you a very nice lunch.

Annual Reports

Annual reports are organized very simply. The good
news is contained up front in the president's message
and ensuing text; the bad news is contained in the footnotes to the financial statement.

You should be aware that for big, widely followed
companies, everything of any substance contained in
the annual report was known to sophisticated investors
months earlier.

Inside Information

It's much easier (although illegal) to make money in the market with inside information than with annual reports.

A Republican I know in the executive suite at a major insurance company called a close friend of his in a distant city (a Democrat) and told him to buy all he could of a company then selling at $6 a share. Several days later, the insurance giant tendered for the company at $10 a share. The Republican and the Democrat quietly split the profit. A lot of money is made this way on Wall Street, hard though the SEC tries to prevent it.

Or say you are a trader with a major firm and you get a call from one of the big banks asking you to buy 250,000 shares of Digital Equipment. That is a lot of stock. It will in all likelihood move the price of Digital Equipment up a point or two, at least temporarily. You have this friend somewhere you owe a favor and, when you bump into him, you mention that Digital sure looks good for a quick move. He buys options on the stock and makes 30% on his money in two days. Now he owes you a favor.

Unfortunately, very few investors are anywhere near close enough to the center of financial power ever to be tempted by genuine inside information.

Charts

Charts look like they should work, but they don't. Everybody uses them anyway, just as everyone consults astrology columns in newspapers. Some people even take them seriously. Much good may it do them. The various precepts, strategies, systems, rules of thumb, and general folklore that chart readers espouse have been rigorously tested. To quote Malkiel: "The results reveal conclusively that past movements in stock prices cannot be used to foretell future movements [any more than past flips of a coin will help determine the next flip]. The stock market has no memory. The central proposition of charting is absolutely false, and investors who follow its precepts [as many do] will accomplish nothing but increasing substantially the brokerage charges they pay. Yes," Malkiel writes, "history does tend to repeat itself in the stock market, but in an infinitely surprising variety of ways that confound any attempts to profit from a knowledge of past price patterns."

Nonetheless, chartists are likely to be right about as often as they are wrong, and so constantly find new reason to believe in their craft. Their bookshelves bulge.

Don't waste your time.

Splits

Splits are accorded great excitement on Wall Street. Before the split you had just 200 shares of the stock, at $40 each ($8,000), and now—presto—you have *400* shares of the stock, at $20 each (still $8,000). Nothing has happened; your share of the pie is exactly what it was. They have changed your dollars for twice as many half-dollars or four times as many quarters or ten times as many dimes.

The advantages corporations hope to gain from splits are: to lower the price of the stock so more people can afford to buy it in round lots; to make it look "cheaper"; to increase the number of shares outstanding, and hence the trading volume and liquidity of the stock.

While splits can affect a stock's price, at least temporarily, they in no way change a stock's underlying value (or lack thereof).

Stock Dividends

The only difference between a stock dividend and a stock split is that, being a very small split, it is hoped no prospective buyers will even notice that it has taken place.

Stock dividends are under no circumstances to be confused with real dividends. Their (dubious) value is entirely psychological—it is hard to believe that it merits the cost of issuing all those extra little stock certificates and answering the questions of confused shareholders.

Prior to the dividend, 100% of the company was divided among the shareholders. Then, in an attempt to keep those shareholders happy without having to pay them anything, each one is given 5% more shares. Now they have exactly what they had before—100% of the company. It is just divided into smaller pieces.

You pay no tax on a stock dividend, because it adds no value to your holdings. What you hope, however, is that Wall Street will not notice that your company has made this quiet little "split" and, accordingly, will keep paying what it used to pay for each now-slightly-less-valuable share.

Sometimes it actually works.

Dividend Reinvestment Plans

These are not the same as stock dividends. Many big companies give their shareholders the choice of receiving their (real) dividends either in cash or in stock. Either way you have to declare the full amount as income. But if you choose to take stock instead of cash, the company takes your dividend, along with a lot of others, and either goes into the market and buys its own stock for you with your money or else sells it direct to you from the corporate treasury.

The advantage to you is that you are forced to save money you might otherwise have spent—if you consider that an advantage—and you pay no brokerage commission to buy the stock. Often, you even get a 5% discount.

The advantage to the company is that it helps keep the stock up (if purchased in the open market), and is a means of raising new capital without having to pay underwriting fees and going through lengthy SEC prospectus procedures (if sold from the corporate treasury).

Although there is no harm in taking dividends in stock—particularly if we are talking about tiny amounts of money or about dividends on stock held in a Keogh Plan or IRA—it makes more sense for substantial investors to take the cash and then decide the optimum place to put it.

Selling Short

When you sell a stock you don't own, you are "selling short." You do this if you think a stock is likely to go down and you wish to profit from its misfortune. To sell a stock short you instruct your broker to (*a*) "borrow" it from someone who does own it; (*b*) sell it; and then, eventually, (*c*) buy it back—hopefully at a lower price than you sold it for—so that you can (*d*) return it. Buying it back to return it is called "covering" your short position.

Selling short is not un-American, as some people seem to feel; neither is it dramatically more risky than "going long" (buying stock outright). True, a stock you buy can go down only to zero, while a stock you short can go up and up and up forever—but few stocks do.

There are three problems with selling short. First, a relatively small one, is that instead of *receiving* dividends while you sit with your position, you may actually have to *pay* dividends. (You borrowed the stock from some nameless, faceless person who does not even know it's been lent; then you sold the stock; now the company pays a 40-cent-a-share dividend, which the lender naturally expects to receive. Your broker deducts that amount from your account and deposits it in his. Silver lining: any dividends you pay out lower your taxable income.)

Second, by selling short you are in effect betting against the management of a company, who are, doubtless, applying their best efforts to making things turn out all right. They could succeed. (Actually, you are betting that *other investors* have not fully grasped how feeble management's competence really is, or what a mess the company is really in, or how little value and potential really underlies its inflated stock.)

Third and most serious, shorting stocks makes the amateur investor even more nervous than buying them. It is not at all atypical for the small investor to spot a stock that is genuinely worth shorting, short it, begin to go crazy as it climbs yet another 20 points, lose his resolve, and bail out at the top—just days before the bottom falls out.

If you do want to short a stock, never short it "at the market." When you buy or sell "at the market"— an "open order"—you are instructing your broker to pay whatever he has to, or accept whatever he has to, to make the trade. Like sending your child out for a pound of coffee without adding: "But don't buy it if it's more than $4." The alternative to "market orders" are "limit orders." "Buy 100 shares at 38¼ or better," you tell your broker, meaning that 38¼ is the absolute top you will pay.

It is dangerous to short a stock "at the market" because there is a rule about short sales: you may only short stock on an "uptick"—that is, when the price is higher than the "last different price at which it traded." If the stock is falling apart fast, it can be some time before there is an uptick. You wanted to short it at 29½, but placed a "market order"; it trades at 29¼, 29¼, 29⅛, 28⅞, then a block at 28½, more at 28⅛, a big block at 27⅜, more at 27¼, 27⅛, 26⅞,

100,000 shares at 26, and then, finally, somebody bumps it up to 26⅛—an uptick—and that is where your broker calls to tell you that you shorted the stock. (Had you simply been selling it rather than shorting it, you would have made the sale at around 29¼.)

Place a limit on all short sales. Instruct your broker to sell at some figure—say 29 *"or better"*—so that you don't wind up making a trade you wish you hadn't.

Special Offerings

From time to time you may be called upon by your broker to benefit from a "special offering," also known as a "spot secondary." Special offerings are one of the few times where you should consider selling short. Simply put, the special offering is a way of unloading onto the public stock that none of the big professional money managers wants to touch. This is done *not* by giving the public a good break on the price of the stock, in the great tradition of the white elephant sale, but rather by giving the retail broker a fat incentive to push the stuff on his clients—in the great tradition of the hype.

When the broker calls to sell you National Hypothetical—fine company though it may be—don't buy, *sell.* He will stress that you will incur no brokerage fee if you buy the stock—the seller has generously agreed to pick up the tab—but short it anyway. If the stock hasn't fallen nicely within a week or two, cover the short and call it a day. But in most cases, the stock does fall. Cover your short and pocket a quick profit.

Although special offerings are not as common now as they were in the worst of the bear market, a broker did alert me to one just as I was beginning this chapter. Sixty-seven thousand shares of Witco Chemical. Witco, a sound and prosperous company, had been selling around 32 up until a few days before the offering; the stock was being offered at 30 (of which the seller would receive only about 28½, the rest going to the brokerage house and the broker).

With a special offering there is no prospectus, no advance warning so investors can study the situation carefully—it's hit-and-run, done overnight and into the next day. The stock continues to trade on the floor of the New York Stock Exchange while brokers are trying to unload their special block off the Exchange.

Witco, indeed, was selling at around 29½ on the open market, a couple of hundred shares at a time, while the brokerage firm was pushing 67,000 shares onto its clients at 30. I managed to short 300 shares at 29⅜. Within a day or two it was 28¾. Then quarterly earnings were announced: $1.09, versus $1.22 for the year-earlier quarter. (Is it possible the sellers of 67,000 shares had an inkling?) Two days later the stock was 26¼ (I covered at 26¾). In the fullness of time, the stock might perform well, but the clients who had bought the week before at 30—"Have I got a deal for you!"—couldn't have been too pleased.

One reason stocks go down after special offerings is that the people in such a hurry to sell sometimes have a reason. The other is that such a big sale sops up a lot of demand for a stock, leaving a preponderance of potential sellers and a dearth of potential buyers.

I devote so much space to special offerings not because they occur very often, which they don't, but as an example of what reputable brokers will do, if necessary, to earn commissions. All 67,000 shares of Witco were sold at 30.

The Counter

If there is really a counter somewhere, I have never seen it. "Over-the-counter" is an arena of stocks too small to be (or just not interested in being) traded on a stock exchange. Instead of there being an "auction" market for these stocks, where buyers and sellers meet to do business, there are dealers who keep them in inventory. You want some, we got some.

The problem with O-T-C stocks, particularly if you're not planning to buy and hold for the long haul, is that in addition to brokerage commissions you have the "dealer spread" to contend with. The dealer spread, in percentage terms, is generally enormous. A stock may be quoted 4½ bid, 5½ asked. That means you have to pay the dealer $550 for 100 shares, plus a commission to your broker; and then you can turn around and sell him the same 100 shares for $450, *minus* a commission for the broker. Although that is about as extreme as the spreads get, and although your broker can often do a little better for you than the listed quote, it is still very discouraging. In this example the stock has to rise from 4½ bid to about 6 bid—a 33% gain—for you just to break even.

While you should not rule out O-T-C issues, you must take these often enormous "transaction costs" fully into account before investing.

Portfolio

You have heard of a pride of lions, a medley of ducks, a bevy of quail? So, too, a portfolio of stocks and bonds.

Beta

Beta is a measure of a stock's volatility. When the market goes up, does this stock tend to go up faster? Or not as fast? When the market is falling, does this stock plunge? Or does it just drift downward? The more speculative the stock (or portfolio), the higher its beta. If it moves twice as wildly as the market—a

10% decline in the market produces a 20% decline in the stock—its beta is 2. If it moves only half as forcefully—a 10% market gain produces only a 5% gain in the stock—then its beta is 0.5. Most stocks move about like the market, so, give or take a little, most stocks have betas around 1.

It doesn't take calculus to know that utilities are relatively stodgy and that hot technology stocks are more speculative. But beta quantifies it. "What's your portfolio's beta?" you can ask showoff friends to put them in their places. On the off-chance they have any idea, you should react this way:

> If beta is under 1: "Playing it safe this year, eh?" (Particularly biting if the market has recently been zooming.)
>
> If over 1: "Looking for a good run in the market, are you?"

Beta late than never.
You beta believe it.

The Dow Jones Industrial Average

Against all reason, this highly unscientific average of 30 stocks is the most widely followed "financial barometer"—and probably always will be, which is why, reluctantly, I have referred to it throughout this book. (To see where it's been lately, in broad strokes, see the graph on page 133. It shows, as well, how the Dow has fared *adjusted for inflation*.)

The Dow is a conservative index. When the market goes down, it tends to go down less; when the market goes up, it tends to go up less. Relative to the market as a whole, it has a low "beta."

There are many other indices to look at if you are so inclined, such as the New York Stock Exchange composite index. Possibly the easiest way to compare the

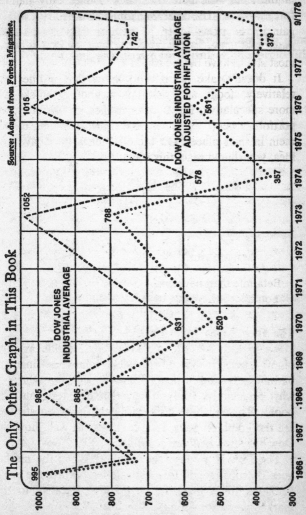

The Only Other Graph in This Book

Source: Adapted from Forbes Magazine.

DOW JONES
INDUSTRIAL AVERAGE

DOW JONES INDUSTRIAL AVERAGE
ADJUSTED FOR INFLATION

progress of small bottom-tier companies with the Dow is to follow the American Exchange (Amex) index.

In 1974 and 1975, the Amex index was almost identical to the Dow, only 10 times smaller. When the Dow was 830, the Amex index was between 80 and 85; when the Dow was 911, the Amex index might be 91 or 92. Why not "split" the Amex index 1 for 10, I once suggested? This would make it easily comparable with the Dow and draw more attention to the Amex, which the Amex sorely needed. The index remains unsplit, but I continue to add a zero to it and compare it with the Dow. At this writing, multiplied by 10, it has climbed to around 1650; the Dow is sitting around 880. Amex stocks are less ignored than they were in 1974–75.

Leverage

Leverage is very boring to write about, because no matter how you attack it, you wind up saying what everyone else says, always, without variation, as sure as the caution on every pack of cigarettes: ". . . but be careful—leverage works both ways."

Leverage is buying a house for $50,000—$10,000 down with a $40,000 mortgage—and selling it the year after for $70,000. That's not a 40% profit ($20,-000 on top of $50,000)—it's a 200% profit ($20,000 on $10,000). The difference is leverage. You make a profit on not just your own money, but also on all the money you borrowed.

Leverage can obviously improve your return on investment. But be careful—leverage works both ways. If you had to sell the house for $40,000—20% less than you paid for it—you'd have just enough to pay back the bank, but not a penny of your own cash left. You would have lost not 20% on the transaction, but 100%.

Margin

Margin is how brokerage firms make it easy for you to over-extend yourself with leverage. They do this by lending you the money to buy more stock than you otherwise could. It's not unlike the credit card a department store will gladly issue, only more profitable for the issuer. On small sums the brokerage house will typically charge you 2% more than the banks charge them. Since they hold your stock in their computer as security, they take no risk. If your securities decline in value anywhere near enough to jeopardize the loan, you either ante up more security, or else your position is sold out, like it or not, before it can deteriorate any further. (Of course, it is just when others are having their positions sold out from under them at distress prices that you should be in there buying.)

Some discount brokers take a smaller interest bite. The same month my full-rate broker was charging 7¼%, my discount broker charged 6%.

Margin Calls

A margin call is what alerts you to the fact that your life is going to hell and that you *never* should have gotten into the market when you did, let alone on margin.

Options

One way to get incredible leverage is with options.

As if the stock market weren't already enough like Caesar's Palace, someone decided the real action would be in trading not stocks, but options. He was right.

Own a stock and you could wait years before it doubles. Buy an option and it can double overnight.

Own a stock and you own a small portion of a company's assets and earning power. Buy or sell an option, and you are placing a bet—nothing more.

Options, therefore, are a great deal more fun than stocks, more potentially lucrative, and more likely to wipe you out. Brokers love them.

If you know which way a stock is going to go, you can make a fortune with options. *But the stocks on which options are traded are, necessarily, the most widely followed and intensively analyzed ones . . . the ones most likely to conform to the random walk theory of price movement.* The hardest ones to outguess. That being the case, the odds in this game are with your broker.

This doesn't mean that I personally have summoned the willpower to abstain from the options market, or that I would pass up for any sum the opportunity to tell you about the time I bought Merrill Lynch options at ⅜.

There I was in the Beverly Hills Hotel, in one of the smaller suites (a converted maid's room), charged with writing a story about the litigation over the remake of *King Kong* ("the most exciting original motion picture event of all time"), but thinking, instead, about Merrill Lynch.

It was the first week in January 1976, and the market had suddenly begun to go wild. Volume on the New York Stock Exchange, which had been running at an unspectacular 15 or 18 million shares a day —only marginally more exciting than the 11- and 12-million-share days during the worst of the dark days of '74 and '75—was suddenly hitting 30 million shares. Party to each trade, I knew, were a buyer, a seller— and a broker.

Merrill Lynch stock was selling for around 16½. For some reason it had not yet reacted to the surge in volume. It seemed to me that if the volume kept up, Merrill Lynch stock would rise. So I bought 10 Merrill Lynch April 20s. Which means I purchased 10 options, at 100 shares an option, to buy Merrill Lynch stock at $20 a share (the "strike price"), any time between then and April.

The right to buy a stock for 20 when it is selling at 16½ is not tremendously valuable, so it cost me just ⅜ of a dollar per share—$37.50 per 100-share option—$375 in all. Plus $76.88 in commissions.

Stock market volume continued to surge.

Merrill Lynch stock began to move up.

My options began to move up with it.

God, it was thrilling!

As the stock passed 20, the "strike price," the option was being traded at 1½. This was the "premium" people were paying for the chance that Merrill Lynch would go still higher before April (possibly much higher), and that the option would thus actually be *worth* something.

The price I had paid for this option was ⅜. Now it had quadrupled—1½.

I sold two of my options for $300—almost as much as I had paid for all 10. I did this because I am a chicken.

Stock market volume continued to set records. Why this was happening I had no idea.

I sold two more options at 1¾.

Another at 2¹¹⁄₁₆.

Two more at 3⅛.

Another at 3⅜ (Merrill Lynch stock was now trading around 22½).

Another at 5½—$550 for an option that had cost me $37.50.

And, finally, the last at 6.

Total investment: $375. Time elapsed: one month. Profit after commissions (but before taxes): $2,397.67.

Options have a certain allure.

Indeed, had I held all 10 until the April expiration date, instead of selling on the way up, I could have turned my $375 into $15,000!

One thing you have to bear in mind, however, is that somewhere there is a person who *sold* me those 10 Merrill Lynch April 20s at ⅜.

I won. He lost. Between the two of us, we generated $500 in brokerage commissions.

Options are what's known as a zero-sum game—for every winner there is an equal and opposite loser—except it's worse than that, because of the brokerage commissions.

Now. The Merrill Lynch options I have been describing are called "calls." They give the purchaser a call on someone else's stock. If you think a stock is going up, you can buy a call on it. If you own a stock and want to earn an extra return from it, you can *sell* a call on it. The option buyer gives a relatively small bird in the hand to the option seller, in return for a long shot at 10 in the bush. It is a redistribution of risk.

If you play the options game as a buyer of calls, you will have some terrific gains, lots of little losses, and lots of brokerage fees. Your broker will stress that you are getting to "control" $16,500 worth of stock (in the case above) for a commission of merely $76.88 —peanuts. But the fact remains that of the $375 you actually invested—your bet—a little over 20% is going to the house. And should you wish to cash in your chips, that's another 20%. The commission rate declines sharply with the size of the trade, but it's never insignificant, even with the largest trades.

Calls are bets that a stock will go up. Puts are bets it will go down. You can buy puts, too.

If you buy a put, you are buying the right to *sell* a stock at a specified price. That right becomes valuable if the stock goes down. Say you buy a General Motors

April 70 put. You have the right to sell 100 shares of GM to me (put it to me, as it were) at 70 any time up until April. You pay me $250 for this right, and GM is selling at 73. Then airbags start misfiring all over the country and it looks as though GM will have to recall all its cars. The market panics and the stock falls to 51. You buy it at 51 and put it to me at 70. You have made 19 points a share, or $1,900—minus commissions and minus the $250 you paid me for the put.

All you stand to lose when you buy a put is the cost of the put. If you had shorted GM instead, and it had gone to 110, you could have lost yourself a lot of money.

We could go on at some length in this vein . . . I have not yet talked of selling puts, just buying them; let alone straddles (buying a put and a call on the same stock at the same time, hoping the stock will make a dramatic move in one direction or another, but not knowing or caring which), spreads (buying an option at one strike price and selling another at a higher or lower strike price), or any of a dozen other arcane strategies one might employ.

Just remember this: it is a zero-sum game and the odds are definitely against you. Anything you do win (and lots of people do) is fully taxed as a short-term capital gain. There are no dividends, lots of commissions. It may be addictive.

Commodities

Again? I thought we'd disposed of commodities in the first chapter.

Well, yes—but there is no end to the persistence of the nation's commodities salesmen. I once wrote a very negative column on commodities for *Esquire*. In the ensuing weeks, six different commodities salesmen from as far off as Arkansas (that one touting coffee) called

—not to complain, but to try to sell me commodity futures. (What inside dope on coffee they have in Arkansas I can hardly imagine.)

To reinforce your resolve, I quote from investment veteran John Train's forthcoming book on great investors (Harper and Row):

Stanley Kroll spent 13 years as a commodity broker. He had about 1,000 nondiscretionary customers [customers who made their own decisions with or without his advice]. . . . He even wrote a book on commodity trading. Stanley Kroll says that none of his original 1,000 customers made money. Not one. . . . Kroll and the other commodity specialists I've talked to agree that the retail commodity speculator will almost always sooner or later lose his money, as infallibly as if he cranked away day and night at a slot machine.

And yet away they crank.

Tax Shelters

Tax shelters, other than the ones described in Chapter 4, are not the sweet deals many people imagine. At best, tax shelters merely postpone taxes—they do not eliminate them.

Moreover, tax shelters frequently go awry. Some are outright frauds; others are well-intentioned ventures that fail (as in the case of an oil well that comes up dry); and still others do not stand up to IRS scrutiny at audit time.

There are, of course, a great many legitimate tax shelter deals, principally in real estate and oil-and-gas. A few even manage the feat of converting ordinary income into lower-taxed capital gains. But apart from the difficulty of telling the good ones, which are rare, from the rotten ones, which abound, there is the problem that the good ones rarely accept participations of less than $20,000 or $25,000. Which may be just as well, because *only individuals in the highest tax bracket (or soon to be in a lower one) should even consider tax shelters.*

The mistake many people make is to shelter income that might have been taxed at, say, 40 or 45% in the current year, only to see it added to their taxable income a year or two later—and to have it taxed, because the tax rate is graduated, at an even higher rate. Some wealthy but ill-advised individuals have actually managed to take "earned income," subject to a maximum 50% federal tax, and, through a "tax shelter," convert it to investment income that under current law may be taxed as high as 70%.

There are other pitfalls as well—ask your accountant about the woes of "recapture" and the agonies of the "preference tax," for starters. But as a rule of thumb, you should simply know that taxpayers with gross incomes under $60,000 or $80,000 are unlikely to benefit from tax shelters.

Those who might benefit can find out about prospective shelters from many brokerage firms, as well as lawyers and accountants who deal with wealthy individuals. But before signing on, seek out the best possible tax and legal advice (no small expense in itself). What's more, investors should satisfy themselves that the prospective deal, even *apart* from its purported tax advantages, is an attractive one. Because no matter how you slice it, in the long run it is very hard to come out ahead by losing money.

Real Estate

One "tax shelter" that does make sense for the typical family is a home. Houses have been appreciating a lot faster than stocks over the last decade. And even if that does not hold true for the next one, houses are likely at least to be good hedges against inflation. The higher your tax-bracket, the more of the carrying costs Uncle Sam shoulders by virtue of the tax deductions home-ownership provides. Meanwhile, paying off the mortgage provides a good method of "forced saving." Your equity builds month by month, albeit very slowly in the early years. And if the value of your property does keep pace with inflation, you come out way ahead. You are making money on your own money, but also— leverage—on the money the bank lent you.

After becoming their own landlords, the step many enterprising investors take is to become landlord to someone else. For high-tax-bracket investors with the business sense and inclination, buying commercial or residential properties can be very rewarding. Here you get to deduct not just taxes and interest, but depreciation and operating expenses as well. (Depreciation is the key to real estate tax shelters, because while you are deducting it from your taxes the property may actually be *ap*preciating, instead.)

This kind of real estate tax shelter—where you know the area personally, search for your own investment, and are intimately involved in structuring the deal and overseeing the property—is far different from the kind of tax-shelter deal referred to above, where you are one of any number of "limited partners" who, come tax time, will sign just about anything put in front of them that promises to defer taxes. The hand-tailored approach takes a lot more effort; but, done carefully, is less likely to go wrong.

Real estate, indeed, can be as much a part-time *job* —scouting for properties, arranging their purchase, fixing them up, interviewing tenants, keeping them happy, negotiating the bureaucratic maze, cajoling plumbers in emergencies—as an investment. Some people see only headaches and risks. Others see a chance to be creative, to build sizable equity (and even more sizable bank debt), and to run their own show. If you are one of the latter, there are a great many primers available, not to mention eager real estate brokers who may go so far as to offer to manage your properties for you (for a percentage of the rent). One simple place to get an overview is the January, 1978, issue of *Money* magazine ("Waiting Out Profits in Rental Real Estate" by Jeremy Main) which should be available in most libraries. Similarly, the Personal Business Supplement in the May 15, 1978, *Business Week*.

I would only add this caution: it is just when investments have been certified "sure-fire" by the general public, as real estate has, that they may have peaked. (Remember the stock market in 1968?) In many cases, real estate prices have been bid up faster than rents can keep pace, narrowing the return to landlords. Furthermore, the whole game is predicated on continued strong inflation. A fair bet, but not a sure one.

Tax Timing

It is common advice that you not let tax considerations interfere with investment decisions. Don't wait for a gain to go long-term, in other words, if it is likely to evaporate in the meantime.

Nonetheless, tax considerations are very much part of the game and it is foolish to ignore them entirely if you are in a reasonably high marginal tax bracket.

As of 1978, you must have held an asset for a year and a day before any profit you realize selling it can qualify as a long-term capital gain. In the simplest terms, which I will complicate momentarily:

Short-term gains	fully taxed
Long-term gains	only half taxed*
Short-term losses	fully deductible†
Long-term losses	only half deductible†

---

*As this book went to press, it appeared that 6% of long-term capital gains realized after November 1, 1978, would be excluded from income tax, rather than the current 50% exclusion.

†Whether you itemize deductions or not, but in any case only up to a maximum of $3,000 a year. Any excess may be carried over to future years.

All other things being equal, therefore, one wishes all gains to be long-term and all losses short-term. That way, if it were not for the Spoiler, one could make an after-tax profit just by breaking even. In the 50% bracket, a $3,000 long-term capital gain would net out to $2,250 after tax; while a $3,000 short-term loss would be 50% absorbed by tax savings—$1,500 after tax. Net after-tax profit: $750.

Unfortunately—the Spoiler—this doesn't work if the gain and loss are realized in the same year. The government makes you net out one against the other. Only against the *net* gain for the year may you apply the long-term-gain tax benefit.

The government is very unfair about this, but such is life. (Equally unfair: If you make a big profit, it's fully taxed, but if you suffer a big loss, only $3,000 of it is deductible against any year's income. Where is justice?)

So the real trick is not only to try to keep your losses short-term and your gains long-term to the extent that it's practical to do so, but to take them in different years in order to get the full tax benefits of each.

Realized in any given year	Tax consequences
Long-term gains and long-term losses	OK—the tax advantage of the former cancels out the disadvantage of the latter
Short-term gains and short-term losses	OK—they cancel out
Long-term gains and short-term losses	Lousy—the tax advantages are wasted on each other
Short-term gains and long-term losses	Swell—the tax disadvantages of each cancel each other out

Because short-term losses provide more of a tax saving than long-term losses, it may make sense to sell a loser before it becomes, irrevocably, long-term.

The problem is: if the stock represented good value when you bought it, it might well represent even better value now that it is substantially lower in price. So what you might do is sell it to establish the short-term tax loss—and then buy it right back again. The IRS, however, requires that you wait 31 days before reversing a sale—otherwise they call it a "wash" and pretend, for tax purposes, that it never took place.

So, if you calculate that your tax savings will justify the out-and-back-in brokerage commissions, you could sell the stock to establish your loss, then buy it back 31 days later.

Or, if you have this unreasoning terror that the stock will take off during those intervening 31 days, as it could, you can do it the other way around. Buy a second 100 shares (or whatever number you were holding) first; then wait 31 days and sell the first 100 for the short-term tax loss.

The day you buy a stock, enter a note in your calendar 10 months hence to reevaluate it before it goes long-term; and keep a running tally of your long- and short-term gains and losses as you realize them in any taxable year, so you know where you stand at any given time in making these kinds of decisions.

It's impossible to try to figure out in January or February where you are likely to be, taxwise, near the end of the year (unless you have massive tax-loss carryovers from past years); so in the early months of the year you can pretty much let the chips fall as they may. But by the latter third of the year, taxes should be at least one of the factors you consider when you are thinking of selling—or holding—stocks. Not an overriding consideration, by any means, but a real one.

Keeping taxes in mind as you pursue your investments can save you hundreds of dollars a year.

To summarize:

1. Try not to waste the tax benefits of short-term losses on long-term gains—and vice versa.

2. Don't take a short-term gain when, by waiting just a little longer, it would turn long-term—unless you have a very good reason. (However, if you have already realized substantial losses during the year, it doesn't make any difference.)

3. When you are considering selling for a short-term tax loss, consider buying back the same number of shares 31 days later (or earlier). Otherwise, you could get into the habit of buying high and selling low.

Examples:

Dumb

You have no other gains or losses and in November you sell at a substantial profit a stock you bought in January. *Dumb!* Had you waited a few more weeks, your gain would have been long-term, taxed only half as heavily—and taxed in the following year.

Dumb

You have already realized lots of gains and losses during the year, but so far the sum of your short-term gains ($2,200) and losses ($4,300) is a $2,100 short-term loss. The sum of your long-term gains ($400) and losses ($125) is a $275 long-term gain. OK. What's done is done. Now you are nearing the end of the year and you decide to take (cash in) a $1,500 long-term gain. *Dumb!* The potential tax benefit of the long-term gain is wiped out by your short-term losses. Unless you have a strong reason to sell, why not wait a little longer and take the gain next year, when you might not have losses? Taking the gain now just serves to increase your taxes.

Smart

You have a big tax-loss carry-forward from prior years, when you had more losses than could be deducted in any given year. You also have a long-term gain in a stock that's been going up like crazy, and you'd just as soon not waste its potential tax benefits by having it netted out against the loss. But your stock has just hit the cover of *Time* magazine and it appears to you quite likely that the jig is up: it looks so good, it must be the top. You say to hell with the tax consequences, sell the stock for a handsome gain, and take the wife and kids to the best restaurant in town.

The Only Other Investment Guides You Might Want to Read.

As I said in Chapter 1, even if this is the only investment guide you'll ever need, it is hardly the only one that's any good. To get an idea of how difficult it is to beat the market, and for a very readable tour of the stock market: *A Random Walk Down Wall Street* by Burton Malkiel (Norton, 1973). For a different slant: *Psychology and the Stock Market: Investment Strategy Beyond Random Walk* by David Dreman (Amacom, 1977). The classic of stock selection, the bible of security analysis: *The Intelligent Investor* by Benjamin Graham (fourth revised edition, Harper & Row, 1973); if you really are going to scour balance sheets for stocks selling well beneath their underlying "value," this is the book. Another thoughtful guide: *Jackpot* by Robert Metz (Simon & Schuster, 1977).

But remember, the more time you spend reading about the stock market, the more you are likely to want to try your hand. Are you sure this is where you want to put your money? Are you sure you want to begin devoting a good portion of your waking, worrying life in pursuit of this hobby? Have you the temperament to succeed? Can you afford to lose? Have you made out well with past sorties into the market?

CHAPTER 8

What to Do If You Inherit a Million Dollars; What to Do Otherwise

> All I want is a room somewhere,
> Far away from the cold night air.
> With one enormous chair—
> Oww wouldn't it be loverly?
> Loverly—loverly.
>
> —*My Fair Lady*

As television viewers of the fifties all know, coming into a million dollars, even if it is tax-free, is not all applause and confetti. In fact, it can cause all kinds of inner demons to surface.

Listen to Gail Sheehy, author of the huge bestseller *Passages*. Did coming into money cause her any problems?

"Yeees!" she cries plaintively. "It makes me sweat a lot more, it makes me embarrassed and guilty—I mean, truly, it's terrible.

"It's much more fun being the aspirant, because once you have gotten there, even if you are just there temporarily (as you must continually remind yourself you are), you're in a position of defending or protecting rather than aspiring or building.

"It's terribly uncomfortable. It's also a problem that is *totally* unsympathetic to anyone who has 5 cents less than you do. Right? I mean, it's hardly one of the Neediest Cases. So there's nobody you can talk to."

When it first became clear that *Passages* had hit the jackpot, Sheehy was chatting with Random House editor Jason Epstein. Said he: "Yes, well. Money. You will find, Gail dear, that it will now be a dull ache in the back of your head. For*ever*."

"It was so ominous," Gail says, "and it was exactly how I felt!"

Sheehy has been rich and Sheehy has been, if not poor, nearly so. "I can't say that I was happiest when I was living in a fourth-floor walkup on East Seventh Street with a one-year-old baby, you know, carting her on one hip and the wash on the other when I came home from work." But neither is she now laughing all the way to the bank.

Many of us, needless to say, would have an easier time than Gail Sheehy "coping" with a fast million. Or think we would. Or would love at least the chance to try.

Still, the problem with sudden wealth seems less how to invest it than how to keep it from wrecking your life. You will notice that in movies and novels where the hero actually manages to pull it off—to steal, win, or discover a fortune—they always end the action there. As if to say that the happiness with which they lived ever after goes without saying. When, in fact, the real story is that the screenwriter or novelist knows full well that this is not true, and can't think of a thing to write that wouldn't be anticlimactic.

Sheehy, with great good sense, is trying hard to avoid what she calls "that classic American trap—which is, you suddenly get a windfall and then, instead of living pretty much as you have, only a little better and with a lot more security behind you—with money there to do something amazing every once in a while when it really counts—you suddenly leap up to meet that income level and always bubble up over it, and then are constantly running to keep up with this tremendous overhead you've established." It is the financial equivalent of the Peter Principle—getting yourself in, no matter how much you have, just a little too deep for comfort.

What to do, then, should you have the ill fortune to inherit a million dollars?

1. Consult a good tax attorney. You can afford it. Explore, particularly, whether there are trusts you should set up for your dependents.

2. Put a large portion of the money—say, 60% —into a diversified portfolio of bonds of varying maturities and varying grades. Municipals or taxables, whichever will provide the highest after-tax yield. (You can switch from one to the other should your tax bracket change significantly.)

3. Buy a bigger house, if you want one, or a country place—but not so big that the cost of carrying it will in any way strain the flow of fixed income from your bond portfolio.

4. Put most of the rest into two dozen stocks of the type described in Chapter 5. Good values. Or into two or three no-load mutual funds.

5. If you must, put 2% of the money into government-issued gold coins, keeping most of them in a bank vault and a few in a very good hiding place at home. This is your rich man's disaster hedge—a reasonable form of insurance, but unlikely to be a good investment.

6. Be sure your will is in order and kept up to date.

7. Now relax and forget the whole thing. Review it, at most, once a year. Make changes only if your tax circumstances change. Reinvest part of the income each year, and enjoy the rest.

This is not necessarily the way to get every last dollar from your inheritance—but isn't not-having-to-try one of the luxuries that having a million should bring?

Unless you want to switch from being whatever you were being to being a financier; unless you enjoy worrying about money and taking risks and paying taxes on profits and stewing over losses; unless you are intrigued by the machinations of the Fed's Open Market Committee and the effects on the financial markets of the latest fiduciary fad—you should simply structure your assets, should you be so fortunate as to have them in such abundance, so as to give you security, peace of mind, and a good eternal income.

Life is not a business, as my father is fond of saying. Why not set yourself up comfortably and stop worrying?

That's what I plan to do when the man from the contest-judging organization calls up to tell me that by placing my YES! token in the "No, I don't wish to purchase any of these magazines but would like to enter the Sweepstakes anyway" slot I have won first prize. (That will be the day.)

Now what to do in the meantime.

Mutual Funds

Far more practical for many investors than trying to go it alone in the stock market—which is at the very least time-consuming, and possibly a good deal worse for those of us with a touch of the self-destructive in our natures—is the no-load mutual fund.

If stocks are appropriate for an investor, and they may not be, as I have stressed repeatedly throughout this book, then no-load mutual funds may be the best way to go about buying them.

Admittedly, for many investors—even if they do

well—profits are only part of the objective. Much of the reward is the fun—challenge—intrigue—of the game itself. I am an investor, and I am the first to admit it. But that's not called investing, strictly speaking. It's called playing.

"The prudent way is also the easy way," counsels Paul Samuelson, nationally renowned economist, in a column he wrote for *Newsweek*. Someone else does the research, someone else does the worrying, someone else holds your certificates and provides a record of your dividends and capital gains for tax purposes. ". . . What you lose is the daydream of that one big killing. What you gain is sleep."

Mutual funds provide the small investor with wide diversification and lower transaction costs (because commissions on large trades are much lower than on small ones). Most allow periodic investments of as little as $25, which is perfectly suited to a monthly savings plan. Most are also geared to set up Keogh and IRA accounts with a minimum of paper work and expense. Not for nothing have millions of Americans chosen to stick with their mutual funds despite the dismal performance of the recent past. (Remember—when things seem most dismal, that's the time to get in.)

With mutual funds the risks of the stock market are still there. Many funds declined 60% and more after the speculative binge of the late sixties and/or in 1973–74. But at least you don't have to make all the foolish decisions yourself. You need only decide which funds to invest in, how much, and when. (See Chapter 5, Rules 1–3.) In this very real sense, you are still managing your own money.

The first step in choosing among mutual funds is about the only one that is at all clear-cut. There are funds that charge initial sales fees of as much as 8.5%, known as the "load"; and there are others that charge no load. *Choose a no-load fund.* To do otherwise is to throw money out the window.*

Statistical studies show that no-load funds perform just as well (and as badly) as load funds. This stands to reason, because that enormous load goes not toward superior management of the fund, but to the salesmen who sell it. And they have no influence on its performance.

Load funds are on the wane as people wise up, but there are still brokers who would love to sell you shares in one; and as long as there are people out selling, there will be people in buying. Don't be one of them.

(If you already own shares in a load fund, the load alone is no reason to sell—you've already paid it. But neither is it a reason not to sell. What's lost is lost.)

In choosing a no-load fund, there are several things to consider. Two things to look at, of course, are the management fee and administrative expenses. These annual charges can be as little as .5% or, with a small fund that can't spread its overhead over a great deal of money, as much as 3% or more. You have to have a very good reason to go with a fund that charges much more than 1% a year for its management and administration. (Many funds will advertise their low management fee without mentioning the annual expenses that are charged as well. Be sure to dig for this number in the prospectus—or ask about it.)

What really matters, of course, is not what a fund will charge you, but what it will *earn* for you. Here you can be much less certain.

Tracked over several up and down cycles in the stock market and graded from A to F on the basis of their relative performance, many funds will rank A or B in bull markets—but D or F in bad ones. This is

---

*An 8.5% load is even worse than it sounds. When you send $1,000 to such a fund, you give up $85 in commissions, so that you are really paying $85 to invest $915—fully 9.3%.

not because the managers are brilliant some years and dunces in others, but rather because these funds have highly volatile (high-"beta") stocks in their portfolios. Other funds, the less volatile ones, are most likely to rank C or D in up markets, as their stocks climb in the "slow lane" relative to others, but B or A in bad markets, when they merely slip while others slide, tumble, or plunge.

You can see, then, how dangerous it is to choose a fund based on its recent performance, as many people do. They buy a fund that has performed even better than the bull market—at the very time that the bull market is petering out and the fund is shifting from its A-rating to its F-rating.

If you knew which way the market was headed at any given time, it would be a simple matter of buying the highly volatile funds at the depths of a bear market, just as things were about to turn, and then switching to the conservative funds (or getting out of the market altogether) just as things were peaking.

However, if you do not have this happy facility—as almost no one does—then what you are looking for is that rare mutual fund that does better than average in both up *and* down markets, as a few do. Several of these I have listed in the appendix "Selected Mutual Funds" (page 180), although it must be stressed that *past performance is no guarantee of future performance*. The Japan Fund, for example, has done well through thick and thin in the past—but this is a fund that invests mostly in Japanese securities. As is well known, the Japanese economy has until recently defied virtually any problem. But who is to say that, relative to American securities, Japanese stocks won't fare poorly in the future? Especially now that the dollar seems to have become such a bargain relative to the yen.

Who is to say, in fact, that the money manager most

responsible for a fund's success in a given two- or three-year period is even still at his desk? *People* manage money, after all, not "funds"—and people move on to new and better jobs, or retire.

To get an overview of virtually all the available funds, their records of performance, size, and the like, I strongly recommend the *Mutual Funds Almanac,* published by the Hirsch Organization, Old Tappan, NJ 07675 ($15), an extremely useful, informative guide.

A $10,000 investment in 1972 could have grown in five years to $16,126 in the Charter Fund of Dallas, Texas—or shrunk to $5,081 in the Chase Frontier Capital Fund of Boston, Massachusetts, one alphabetical listing away. Not all mutual funds are alike. Even with mutual funds, and particularly if you choose specialized ones (like the Japan Fund or the Energy Fund), it would pay to diversify.

One kind of no-load mutual fund that particularly bears consideration is the "closed-end" fund. Such funds originally sold a set number of shares to the public, raising, say, $100 million to invest. Then they closed the doors to new money. Investors who wished to cash in their share of the $100 million would sell their shares just as they would sell any stock, through any broker to any investor interested in acquiring such shares. Presumably, if the fund managers had turned the $100 million into $110 million, each share in the fund would be worth 10% more than it was at the outset. Or so everyone assumed. But things are only worth what people will pay for them, and shares in closed-end funds sank to discounts that ranged from a few percentage points up to 30% and more. (A few funds rose to premiums.) As I write this, for example, you can buy a dollar's worth of the assets of the Madison Fund for 74 cents. Or a dollar's worth of the stocks and bonds in the Lehman Fund for 82 cents.

This won't do you much good if the managers of those funds have picked a dreadful assortment of stocks that all collapse—but it's just about as hard to pick bad stocks as good, so that is unlikely. More likely, you will have a dollar working for you in the stock market even though you only had to pay 74 or 82 cents.

The risk is that the discount, irrational to begin with, could widen still further by the time you went to sell your shares. On the other hand, the discount could narrow—which at least makes more sense, even if it's not necessarily more likely to happen.

Ask a broker for more information on these funds, which he can trade like stocks. The Saturday *New York Times* and the Monday *Wall Street Journal* each carries quotations for these funds in a separate box in the financial section, including the discount at which each sells. They are also known as "publicly traded funds."

SERMONETTE

Whether you choose mutual funds or a direct plunge into the stock market, bonds or a savings account; whether you are able to shelter your investments through a Keogh Plan or IRA; and whether you spend now or save to spend later—you will find that, by the prevailing American ethic, anyway, you never have enough.

D. H. Lawrence wrote a wonderful story years ago called *The Rocking-Horse Winner*. "Although they lived in style," Lawrence wrote of his fictional family, "they felt always an anxiety in the house. . . . There was always the grinding sense of the shortage of money, though the style was always kept up. . . . And so the house came to be haunted by the unspoken phrase: *There must be more money! There must be more money!* The children could hear it all the time, though nobody said it aloud. They could hear it at Christmas, when the expensive and splendid toys filled the nursery. Behind the shining modern rocking horse, behind the smart doll's house, a voice would start whispering: 'There *must* be more money! There *must* be more money!' "

One of the children began playing the horses. Before long, in league with the gardener, he had managed to turn a few pennies into a small fortune. The child arranged to have it given to his mother, anonymously. "Then something very curious happened. The voices in the house suddenly went mad, like a chorus of frogs on a spring evening." Debts were paid off and new luxuries lavished—"and yet the voices in the house, behind the sprays of mimosa and almond-blossom, and from under the piles of iridescent cushions, simply trilled and screamed in a sort of ecstasy: 'There *must* be more money! Oh-h-h; there *must* be more money. Oh, now, now-w! Now-w-w—there *must* be more money!—more than ever! More than ever!' "

More is never enough. But there may be a way around this for some people, a way to be just as contented and happy if you don't inherit a million dollars as if you do. It is suggested by this passage from *Stone Age Economics* by Marshall Sahlins:

By the common understanding, an affluent society is one in which all the people's material wants are easily satisfied. . . . [But] there are two possible courses to affluence. Wants may be "easily satisfied" either by producing much or desiring little. The familiar conception, the Galbraithean way, makes assumptions peculiarly appropriate to market economies: that man's wants are great, not to say infinite, whereas his means are limited, although improvable: thus, the gap between means and ends can be narrowed by industrial productivity. . . . But there is also a Zen road to affluence, departing from premises somewhat different from our own: that human material wants are finite and few, and technical means unchanging but on the whole adequate. Adopting the Zen strategy, a people can enjoy an unparalleled material plenty—with a low standard of living.

Or, as a friend of mine said recently: "It's just as easy to live well when you're poor as when you're rich —but when you're poor, it's much cheaper."

This is not to advocate Buddhism, asceticism, spartanism—or, for that matter, poverty. "I been poor and I been rich—and honey, rich is better"—and all that. Naturally. I, for one, like living a little better every year. But it *is* true that, ultimately, how you should spend or invest your money depends not so much on price-earnings ratios or dividend rates as on those larger questions that forever lurk, but generally go unasked: Who am I? What am I trying to do with my life? Is money the means or the end?

There is a good measure of self-knowledge required to choose the proper investment course. It has even been postulated that many small investors in the stock market, without knowing it, secretly want to lose. They jump in with high hopes—but feeling vaguely guilty. Guilty over "gambling" with the family's money, guilty over trying to "get something for nothing," or guilty over plunging in without really having done much research or analysis. Then they punish themselves, for these or other sins, by selling out, demoralized, at a loss.

In any event, whether or not they secretly want to, many investors, failing to seek out value and then hold it patiently, do lose. If this little book saved you several hundred dollars a year—on wine (by the case, on sale), on your next car (seemingly to be bought on time, but actually for cash), on life insurance (term instead of whole; SBLI), on brokerage commissions (trading less often, and with a discount broker), and on taxes (particularly with a Keogh Plan or IRA)—I would be delighted. But if it saved you from getting burned in the stock market, or on even one seemingly surefire "investment" someone was trying to sell you— I would be thrilled!

(I hear, by the way, that the Mexican peso is now very strong, and that you can get a hell of an interest rate south of the border.)

Appendices

Twenty-five Things You Might Not Have Thought of That Could Be Tax-Deductible

1. Abortions

2. Face lifts, hair transplants, and other cosmetic surgery

3. Travel to and from your psychiatrist

4. The swimming pool your doctor ordered you to build for the daily regimen you require to avoid paralysis*

5. Calls to your broker—if you make two each business day, $50 a year

6. Calls (from a pay phone or elsewhere) to your modeling agency, agent, secretary, business-related answering service, psychiatrist, and/or attorney (if on business or tax matters)

7. The *Wall Street Journal,* delivered or from the newsstand each morning; *Barron's, Business Week,* trade journals, *Money* (for its tax tips)

8. Diners Club or American Express annual dues, if you can argue that you would not have needed the extra card if it were not for your business entertaining

---

*The amount that may be deducted is the total cost of the pool minus the market value it adds to your home.

9. Postage for business correspondence—to broker, for payment of business bills, etc.

10. Answering service (or machine), if needed for business

11. Full value of stock or real estate you give to charity, even if it has appreciated since you bought it, so long as you have held it more than a year (if you sold it first, you would have to pay long-term capital gains tax on the appreciation)

12. Safe-deposit-box rental (if needed to store securities, tax records, or other business-related material)—and trips to and from

13. Transportation to and from volunteer work, plus expenses

14. Tax-preparation fees

15. Speed-reading course if directly beneficial to current career

16. Installment interest, margin interest, credit card interest—even interest charged by the government itself on late taxes

17. Pocket calculator if purchased for business or taxes or investments (home computer, likewise)—plus batteries

18. Business gifts if given to improve the chances for future sales (up to $25.00 per individual per year)

19. Christmas cards sent to clients, patients, or customers—plus postage

20. Capital losses up to $3,000

21. Equipment or furnishings (typewriters, desks, carpet, copiers, answering machines, etc.) used for

business may be depreciated. *They may also qualify for the investment tax credit,* as well. Write local IRS office for the rules.

22. Sony Betamax, likewise, if bought to tape programs you need to see for business but would otherwise have had to miss

23. Passport fee and passport photo cost if you travel for business

24. Attaché case

25. **Transportation to and from the IRS audit that will almost surely result from your taking deductions such as these**

How Much Life Insurance Do You Need?

Probably more than you can afford. However, you can stretch your coverage by purchasing term instead of whole life, and by shopping for it carefully (see pages 23–5).

Naturally, the amount of life insurance you should carry depends on your circumstances. If you are single with no dependents, you need little—to assist with burial expenses or, posthumously, pay off a few debts —or none. The great push to sell college students life insurance is not entirely unlike the selling of ice to Eskimos, except that a lot more insurance is sold that way than ice.

If you are married, with a hopelessly incompetent spouse, a family history of heart disease, and a host of little children, you should carry a great deal of insurance. Less if your spouse has a reliable income. Less still if you have fewer children or if those children have wealthy and benevolent grandparents. And still less once those children have grown up.

If you are very rich, you need no insurance at all, except as it is helpful in paying off estate taxes. If you *live* richly off a high income but own outright little more than a deck of credit cards and some cardigan sweaters, it will take a lot of insurance to keep from exposing your dependents to an altogether seamier side of life when you are gone.

What you want, ideally, is enough insurance, when

combined with whatever other assets you may have, to pay for what are euphemistically called "final expenses" (deathbed medical expenses not covered by other insurance, funeral expenses, and possible postmortem emergencies like an illness of the surviving spouse, payment of bills you didn't know had been incurred, auto repair, and so on)—and then enough in addition to replace the income you had been kicking into the family till. So that, financially, anyway, you will not be missed.

For final expenses and a cushion for emergencies you will need an amount equal to roughly half one year's gross salary; or, to be on the safe side—particularly if your income is under $15,000—a full year's income.

But that's nothing compared to what you will need to replace your income. Of course, you don't have to replace all of it, just the after-tax portion you were actually taking home. And not even that much, because with you gone, there will be one less mouth to feed, one less theater ticket to buy* . . . Your surviving dependents will need anywhere from 60 to 75% of your current take-home pay in order to live as well, or nearly as well, as they were living before. So if you were earning $30,000 a year and taking home $23,000, your family might maintain roughly the same living standard on $14,000 to $17,000 a year.

A portion of this replacement income will be provided by (tax-free) Social Security benefits. The typical $5,000–10,000 annual benefit a widow with one or more dependent children receives will go a long way toward replacing 60% of the deceased's after-tax in-

---

*Not to mention the savings on commuting expenses, cigarettes, medical and dental expenses, gambling losses, the subscription to *Business Week,* insurance premiums, birthday gifts, Father's (or Mother's) Day gifts, anniversary gifts, charitable contributions, clothing, laundry, golf balls, and toiletries and cosmetics.

come. Thus, low-income families need not rely nearly as much on insurance as higher-income families, so long as they are covered by Social Security.

How much of an "endowment" will it take to make up the gap between Social Security payments and what you actually need? Let's say your take-home pay is $23,000, of which you would like to replace $16,000, and that Social Security would in your case amount to $9,000 (until the children are grown). The gap is $7,000 a year.

If you wanted a large enough "endowment," or "annuity," to pay your surviving spouse $7,000 a year for 20 years, and if we assumed he or she would be able to invest the insurance money to return 6% after taxes, then you would need to carry $80,000 in life insurance. You don't need such a large sum that it will throw off $7,000 a year in interest, forever, because your surviving spouse will not live forever. He or she can gradually eat up the principal as well as the interest. To provide a $7,000 annuity that would last *40* years under the same assumptions would require $105,000. However, if you wanted the $7,000 payment to increase with inflation, and assumed that the "real" rate of interest your spouse could earn on this money, after taxes and after netting out inflation, were 3%, you would need $104,000 to provide $7,000-a-year-plus-enough-to-cover-inflation for 20 years, $162,-000 for 40 years.

The table that follows shows how much life insurance is needed to provide various levels of after-tax annual income for varying lengths of time. It assumes the insurance proceeds will be invested at a mere 3% after taxes, which may approximate the true return, after inflation, your heirs could hope to earn. By assuming an inflation-adjusted interest rate, you are assuring that each $1,000-a-year your heirs receive will be equivalent to $1,000 of today's buying power. Naturally, if you assumed they could earn a higher interest rate, the amount of insurance you would need would decline drastically. To make this point, I have included in parentheses figures that assume an 8% after-tax return. The problem is that unless your heirs are extraordinarily clever in investing these proceeds (or reckless-but-lucky), they will only be able to earn such a high rate if inflation, too, is running at a high rate . . . in which case the value of their payment each year will shrink and shrink.

	How much insurance you must carry to provide . . .			
this much annual income . . .	. . . . for this many years			
	10 years	20 years	30 years	40 years
$1,000	$8,500 ($6,700)	$15,000 ($10,000)	$20,000 ($11,250)	$23,000 ($12,000)
$2,500	$21,000 ($17,000)	$37,500 ($25,000)	$50,000 ($27,500)	$57,500 ($30,000)
$5,000	$42,500 ($33,500)	$75,000 ($50,000)	$100,000 ($55,000)	$115,000 ($60,000)
$7,500	$64,000 ($50,000)	$112,500 ($75,000)	$150,000 ($85,000)	$172,000 ($90,000)
$10,000	$85,000 ($67,000)	$150,000 ($100,000)	$200,000 ($112,500)	$230,000 ($120,000)
$15,000	$128,000 ($100,000)	$225,000 ($150,000)	$300,000 ($170,000)	$345,000 ($180,000)

NOTE: Main entries assume benefits will earn 3% after inflation and taxes; parenthetical entries—8%.

If these figures look overwhelming (and they do), remember that they may be reduced by the value of assets you already own and that the income they will provide sits on top of Social Security benefits. Also, your spouse could remarry; your spouse could go to work; once the children are grown, they could provide support as well. Furthermore, it is not inconceivable that your family could be happy with a more modest life style than they now enjoy.

Nine Simple Steps to Your Answer

1. Determine the 60–75% portion of your current annual take-home pay your family would need to live nicely without you .... _ _ _ (Annual Replacement Needs)

2. Subtract from this the approximate annual Social Security benefit your family would receive if you died today .... − _ _ _ (Annual Social Security)

3. The difference is the annual gap you will want your life insurance to make up .... ═══ (Annual Gap)

4. Using the figure in Step 3 ("Annual Gap"), consult the table on page 169 to find the approximate "endowment" you would need to close this gap for the desired number of years .... _ _ _ ("Endowment" Required)

5. Add to this a provision for "final expenses" equal to 50 or even 100% of a full year's gross salary .... + _ _ _ (Final Expenses)

6. The total of Steps 4 and 5 is the maximum amount of insurance coverage you would need.... _____ (Gross Insurance Needed)

7. From this you should subtract the value of other assets you may own, such as savings accounts, stocks and bonds, a pension or profit-sharing plan at work, a group life insurance policy at work (do not include equity in your home, as you will not want your heirs to have to sell it or to increase the mortgage) .... − _ _ _ (Other Assets)

8. Finally, adjust downward for such intangibles as wealthy grandparents, or a spouse who is resourceful, employable, or likely to remarry. Adjust downward, also, to the extent—if any—you feel your family would be happy with even less than the 60–75% of your current take-home pay you figured on above. If, for example, they could manage in a less expensive home, subtract the difference between what they could get for your present one and what the new one would cost .... − _ _ _ (Intangible Adjustments)

9. This is roughly the amount of life insurance you should, if at all possible, be carrying. Review these calculations as your circumstances change .... ═══ (Net Life Insurance Needed)

Life insurance companies have innumerable plans designed to fit the great variety of personal circumstances that make people's insurance needs differ. While on the one hand it is true you should beware of the insurance man out to sell you the world, it is also true that a competent insurance agent should be able to tailor an insurance program to your own needs. Be certain to get two or three competing sales pitches before you buy. Don't be afraid to ask one agent to comment on another's proposal, and vice versa. And if SBLI is available in your state, see them first.

How To Figure Your
Social Security Benefits

There is no way to know exactly what your Social Security benefits will be when you begin to collect them. However, you can probably get a pretty good idea by looking to see what they would be *now,* were you to retire, die, or become disabled today.

Social Security benefits are likely to rise steadily with the cost of living, it's true. But in *real dollars, real buying power,* it's reasonable to assume that the payments will neither increase (how could we afford it?) nor decrease (how could Congress allow it?) sharply.

The situation is further complicated by the fact that what you will eventually receive in Social Security benefits depends in part on how much you were earning in the years when your employer was deducting Social Security tax (FICA) from your paycheck—or, if self-employed, how much you were paying the government directly. What's more, in the case of death benefits, the payout to your surviving spouse will depend in part on your age at death and the composition of your family.

In other words, the examples on the next page are to be taken as *only the roughest guideline* of what you might expect.

These figures assume, at the low end, that the worker has averaged about $4,000 in Social Security-taxed earnings a year since 1950; and, at the high end, that the worker has in all years earned an amount at least

equal to the top income level at which Social Security
is taxed. (As recently as 1965, only the first $4,800

Examples of Annual Income from Social Security

Recipient	Amount
Worker retiring at 65, or disabled— with no dependents	$4,000– 6,500
Worker retiring at 65, or disabled— with dependents	$7,500–11,000
Widow or dependent widower at 65	$4,000– 6,500
Widow or widower caring for one child	$6,000– 9,500
Widow or widower caring for more than one child	$7,500–11,000

of earnings was subject to Social Security tax. By
1979 the figure had climbed to $22,900. It is slated to
climb to $25,900 in 1980 and $29,700 in 1981.)

To qualify for Social Security benefits, most people
must have had earnings subject to Social Security tax
for a total of 10 years—although for some people who
are retiring soon, and in cases of disability, as little as
1½ years may be required.

If you are within several years of retirement, don't
rely on the rough guidelines above—write or call any
of the 1,300 Social Security offices around the country
and ask for the booklet and forms that will help you
make a closer estimate.

Cocktail Party Financial Quips
to Help You Feel Smug

1. If you are fully invested in the market (or wish to pretend you are), you can say: "I'm betting that the Fed will ease up." This means you think the Federal Reserve Board will ease up on interest rates, allowing them to fall and the stock market, as a consequence, to rise. Either this is the general consensus, in which case you will seem *au courant;* or else it is a contrary opinion, in which case you will appear to be a shrewd man or woman of independent thought. No matter what "the Fed" is really doing, or how little you know of it or care, that you should have an opinion at all is impressive. If someone tries to pin you down, look genuinely uncomfortable—which won't be hard under the circumstances—and say, just a bit mysteriously: "Forgive me, but I'd rather not discuss it just yet."

2. If you've had the good sense to avoid the stock market, but someone asks you what you're into these days, you can say: "Gee, Bill, I really don't have much of a mind for stocks. I know I must be missing out on some terrific opportunities, but I'm happier just sticking to municipals." This will be taken as a display of false modesty—it will be assumed you really do have a mind for stocks—and it will indicate that you are a high-bracket taxpayer of considerable means. You will be envied.

3. Or: "I'll tell you the truth, Phil, I used to play the market until I toted up how much time I was spending on it—you know, the calls from my broker, checking the stock pages, juggling the commodity straddles to save a few tax dollars. I decided I'd rather spend the time with my kids and settle for a sure 8 or 9 percent in bonds." This is bound to make Phil feel guilty.

4. If someone is waxing philosophical about the market, you can say: "The great mistake made by the public is paying attention to prices instead of values." If that raises an eyebrow, because it sounds a bit more formal than you usually sound, you can continue: "C. H. Dow said that back at the turn of the century [which he did], and it's as true now as it was then [which it is]."

5. If someone is boasting about a stock that's really zoomed, you can say: "Gosh, that's terrific! Sounds like it's time to short some."

6. Or (the killer): "By the way—how'd you do in '74?"

Sample Brokerage Commissions

The table opposite shows New York Stock Exchange commission rates prior to May 1, 1975, when rates became "unfixed." Subsequently, big investors were able to negotiate much lower rates on large trades—but the rates charged small investors at most firms have actually gone *up* somewhat from those shown here. Discount brokers use these old fixed commissions as the base from which they offer discounts of up to 75%.

Commissions for trades involving less than $10,000

Stock price	100 shares	200 shares	300 shares	500 shares	1,000 shares
$ 1	$ 9.24 (18%)	$ 18.48 (18%)	$ 27.72 (18%)	$ 46.20 (18%)	$ 92.40 (18%)
$ 5	$18.04 (7%)	$ 36.08 (7%)	$ 54.12 (7%)	$ 81.95 (7%)	$157.73 (6%)
$10	$27.50 (5.5%)	$ 55.00 (5.5%)	$ 73.70 (5%)	$120.47 (5%)	$213.62 (4%)
$15	$34.65 (4.5%)	$ 67.10 (4.5%)	$ 88.55 (4%)	$148.40 (4%)	
$20	$41.80 (4%)	$ 77.00 (4%)	$116.75 (4%)	$176.36 (3.5%)	
$25	$48.95 (4%)	$ 98.11 (4%)	$133.52 (3.5%)		
$40	$63.80 (3%)	$131.65 (3%)		Involves more than $10,000	
$75	$80.73 (2%)				

NOTE: Figures in parentheses represent the *round-trip* brokerage fee you incur in buying, and eventually selling, the amount of stock indicated.

Selected Discount Brokers

The addresses listed below are the main offices of several discount brokers. Some have branch offices in other cities as well. All either have toll-free numbers for out-of-state customers (as listed), or else accept collect calls. Commission schedules vary—find the one that best matches the kind of trading you do. All are insured up to $100,000, most up to $300,000 per account. Compare services also: is margin available? at what rates? what discounts are available on options? how long are you kept waiting on "hold" on a busy day? will the firm hold your securities for you? send you S & P sheets?

Burke, Christensen & Lewis, Inc.
120 South LaSalle Street
Chicago, IL 60603
(800) 621-0392

30–80% off; $23 minimum

Discount Brokerage Corp.
67 Wall Street
New York, NY 10005
(800) 221-4257

70% off; $30 minimum

Icahn & Co., Inc.
25 Broadway
New York, NY 10004
(800) 221-5735

40–60% off; $30 minimum

Letterman Transaction Services, Inc. 567 San Nicholas Drive Newport Beach, CA 92660 (800) 854-3564	30–80% off; $24 minimum
Muriel Siebert & Co. 77 Water Street New York, NY 10005 (800) 221-5846	50% off; $25 minimum
Odd Lots Securities 60 East 42 Street New York, NY 10017 (212) 661-6755— call collect	Discount by negotiation on each trade; $25 minimum
Quick & Reilly, Inc. 120 Wall Street New York, NY 10005 (800) 221-5220	35–50% off; $30 minimum
Source Securities Corp. 70 Pine Street New York, NY 10005 (800) 221-2430	30–75% off; $25 minimum

Selected Mutual Funds

An excellent compendium of more than 600 funds, their records of performance, size, and policies, is the *Mutual Funds Almanac,* available from the Hirsch Organization, Old Tappan, NJ 07675 ($15). It provides exactly the kind of helpful information and advice any prospective mutual fund buyer should have.

The following no-load funds have done reasonably well in up and in down markets. Although this is no guarantee that they will continue to do well, it may be worth your while writing for their prospectuses and latest reports:

Fidelity Equity Income Fund
35 Congress Street
Boston, MA 02109

Financial Industrial Income Fund
P.O. Box 2040
Denver, CO 80201

Guardian Mutual Fund
522 Fifth Avenue
New York, NY 10036

Hamilton Income Fund
3600 South Yosemite
Denver, CO 80237

Mutual Shares Corporation
170 Broadway
New York, NY 10038

Sequoia Fund
540 Madison Avenue
New York, NY 10022

Windsor Fund
P.O. Box 1100
Valley Forge, PA 19482

The performance of one load fund has been so extraordinary as to warrant inclusion, even though other load funds with excellent records are not listed here. It is the Templeton Growth Fund, 155 University Avenue, Toronto M5H 3B7, Canada. (See page 116.) Unfortunately, there is no assurance how many more years Templeton himself will manage the fund.

A few groups of large no-load funds—not necessarily those with the best performance records—offer the added convenience of "telephone switching," which allows investors to transfer money from one fund to another within the "family" just by calling a toll-free number. Thus, if one felt he could foretell the direction of stock prices or interest rates, he could switch from stocks to bonds to short-term instruments, and back. All this can be done while remaining under the tax shelter of a Keogh Plan or IRA. For more information, call these fund families, toll-free:

Dreyfus: 800-835-2246

Fidelity: 800-225-6190

Financial: 800-525-6148

Rowe Price: 800-638-1527

Vanguard: 800-523-7910

Even if you are wrong in calling stock market moves, you will at least not incur huge brokerage fees as you move in and out of the market.

Fun With Compound Interest

If you have not yet learned how to work the compound-interest key on your pocket calculator, but wish to astound your friends anyway, here is how $1 (or any multiple of $1) would grow at varying rates of interest, compounded annually. Compounded daily it would grow even a little faster. Unfortunately, if you are able to earn a very high rate of interest over a long period of time, it is likely to be because inflation is running at nearly as high a rate. *Net of inflation and taxes, it's no cinch to earn 3 to 4% consistently,* let alone any more. Still, it's fun to think about.

How a Dollar Grows *· ·

Year	3%	5%	6%	7%	8%
1	$1.03	$ 1.05	$ 1.06	$ 1.07	$ 1.08
2	1.06	1.10	1.12	1.14	1.17
3	1.09	1.16	1.19	1.23	1.26
4	1.13	1.22	1.26	1.31	1.36
5	1.16	1.28	1.34	1.40	1.47
6	1.19	1.34	1.42	1.50	1.59
7	1.23	1.41	1.50	1.61	1.71
8	1.27	1.48	1.59	1.72	1.85
9	1.30	1.55	1.69	1.84	2.00
10	1.34	1.63	1.79	1.97	2.16
11	1.38	1.71	1.90	2.10	2.33
12	1.43	1.80	2.01	2.25	2.52
13	1.47	1.89	2.13	2.41	2.72
14	1.51	1.98	2.26	2.58	2.94
15	1.56	2.08	2.40	2.76	3.17
20	1.80	2.65	3.21	3.87	4.66
25	2.09	3.39	4.29	5.43	6.85
30	2.43	4.32	5.74	7.61	10.06
35	2.81	5.52	7.69	10.68	14.79
40	3.26	7.04	10.29	14.98	21.72
50	4.38	11.47	18.42	29.47	46.90
100	$19	$132	$339	$868	$2,200
200	$369	$17,292	$115,125	$753,849	$4.8 million

*To see how $3, or $1,000, or any other figure would grow, simply multiply by 3, or 1,000, or that other figure.

10%	12%	15%	20%	Year
$ 1.10	$ 1.12	$ 1.15	$ 1.20	1
1.21	1.25	1.32	1.44	2
1.33	1.40	1.52	1.73	3
1.46	1.57	1.75	2.07	4
1.61	1.76	2.01	2.49	5
1.77	1.97	2.31	2.99	6
1.95	2.21	2.66	3.58	7
2.14	2.48	3.06	4.30	8
2.36	2.77	3.52	5.16	9
2.59	3.11	4.05	6.19	10
2.85	3.48	4.65	7.43	11
3.14	3.90	5.35	8.91	12
3.45	4.36	6.15	10.70	13
3.80	4.88	7.08	12.84	14
4.18	5.47	8.14	15.41	15
6.72	9.65	16.37	38.34	20
10.83	17.00	32.92	95.40	25
17.45	29.96	66.21	$237	30
28.10	52.80	$133	$591	35
45.26	93.05	$267	$1,469	40
$117	$289	$1,083	$9,100	50
$13,780	$83,523	$1.17 million	$82.8 million	100
$190 million	$7.0 billion	$1.4 trillion	$6.9 quadrillion	200

ABOUT THE AUTHOR

ANDREW TOBIAS is the author of *The Funny Money Game* and the bestselling biography of Charles Revson, *Fire and Ice*. He is a graduate of Harvard College and Harvard Business School. A former contributor to *New York* magazine, he is now a contributing editor of *Esquire*.

MONEY TALKS!
How to get it and How to keep it!

☐	12321	MANAGEMENT & MACHIAVELLI by Anthony Jay	$2.50
☐	12768	MONEY: WHENCE IT CAME, WHERE IT WENT by John Kenneth Galbraith	$2.95
☐	11450	THE GAMESMAN: The New Corporate Leaders by Michael Maccoby	$2.75
☐	12009	THE GREATEST SALESMAN IN THE WORLD by Og Mandino	$1.95
☐	12410	THE PETER PLAN by Laurence Peter	$2.25
☐	8728	YOU CAN PROFIT FROM A MONETARY CRISIS by Harry Browne	$2.25
☐	10155	THE MOTHER EARTH NEWS HANDBOOK OF HOME BUSINESS IDEAS AND PLANS	$2.25
☐	12178	THE JOY OF MONEY by Paula Nelson	$2.25
☐	10932	HOW TO BUY STOCKS 6th rev. ed. by Louis Engel	$1.95
☐	12533	THE PETER PRINCIPLE by Peter & Hull	$2.25
☐	12686	THE PETER PRESCRIPTION by Laurence Peter	$2.25
☐	10028	THE RICH AND THE SUPER RICH by Ferdinand Lundberg	$2.75

Buy them at your local bookstore or use this handy coupon:

Bantam Books, Inc., Dept. MSP, 414 East Golf Road, Des Plaines, Ill. 60016

Please send me the books I have checked above. I am enclosing $_____
(please add 75¢ to cover postage and handling). Send check or money order
—no cash or C.O.D.'s please.

Mr/Mrs/Miss_____

Address_____

City_____State/Zip_____

MSP—2/79

Please allow four weeks for delivery. This offer expires 8/79.

Bantam Book Catalog

Here's your up-to-the-minute listing of over 1,400 titles by your favorite authors.

This illustrated, large format catalog gives a description of each title. For your convenience, it is divided into categories in fiction and non-fiction—gothics, science fiction, westerns, mysteries, cookbooks, mysticism and occult, biographies, history, family living, health, psychology, art.

So don't delay—take advantage of this special opportunity to increase your reading pleasure.

Just send us your name and address and 50¢ (to help defray postage and handling costs).

BANTAM BOOKS, INC.
Dept. FC, 414 East Golf Road, Des Plaines, Ill. 60016

Mr./Mrs./Miss_____
(please print)

Address_____

City_____State_____Zip_____

Do you know someone who enjoys books? Just give us their names and addresses and we'll send them a catalog too!

_____

Mr./Mrs./Miss_____

Address_____

City_____State_____Zip_____

Mr./Mrs./Miss_____

Address_____

City_____State_____Zip_____

FC—9/78